AN OLD

An Old Gaffer's Tale

Martin Eve

SEAFARERBOOKS
LONDON

© Seafarer Books 1984
First published by Seafarer Books
10 Malden Road, London N. W. 5

First paperback edition 1991

ISBN 085036 424 8

Typesetting by Heather Hems
The Malt House Chilmark Wilts.

Jacket from a painting by Bert Wright
Maps drawn by Walter Kemsley

Printed by Whitstable Litho,
Millstrood Road Whitstable Kent

to my father

CONTENTS

Acknowledgement

Grateful thanks to those who have contributed to the writing of *Privateer*'s story, especially to the late Rex Pasley; then to all who have given advice and helped to correct my errors, and especially John Scarlett; to all known and unknown friends who have sent me photos: finally, to all those who have encouraged me, especially Pat.

CHAPTER I

Man Meets Boat

Privateer came into my life unobtrusively, through the letter box. There was a mimeographed description and a small snapshot of her, apparently being overtaken by her tender. This had been sent me by the East Coast Yacht Agency, which had put me on their mailing list and were sending me tempting pictures of old gaffers at prices not much more than I had claimed was my limit. The year was 1965 and I was looking for a boat. I had one, or rather a share in one; she was a 10′6″ catamaran, built by my partner, Roy. We had a lot of fun trailing her to the coast and sailing her about the place, but it was beginning to be difficult to fit my three growing children on her limited deckspace and something had to be done.

For the last few years I had been chartering boats from Maldon, usually in April or October when the rates were at their lowest. Our favourite was a Mapleleaf, a sort of family version of a Folkboat, into whose cabin space Roy and I squeezed numerous children. Another of this charter fleet was an old boat with the odd name of *Aslaug,* originally a gaffer, but converted to leg-of-mutton (you could hardly call it Bermuda), and with an enormous expanse of cabin floor. I had dropped tentative hints about the *Aslaug* to her owner, thinking that she might be getting to be below the general standard of his fleet and that he might part with her for a reasonable

1

sum. But the time for this was not ripe, and *Aslaug* stayed in the Charter fleet for another year or two. Meanwhile, I began to take more active steps than dropping hints and started to read the small ads in the yachting magazines. This was what led me to the East Coast Yacht

The Agency were sending me tempting pictures.

Agency, and to the trail of *Privateer*.

Along with the rest of her vital statistics, she was described as being at Frost & Drake's yard, in Tollesbury;

so the next weekend saw me making an early start to be there in good time. I knew Tollesbury, slightly; Roy and I had launched our catamaran there from the hard, and had returned at half tide and sunk waist deep in the mud before getting the cat back on her trailer. Frost & Drake's yard was not hard to find, with the slip alongside the shed, the cradle hauled up by an ancient Austin 12 engine, still housed in its original bonnet. Inside the shed, Des Drake and old Mr Frost were building a fishing boat. *Privateer,* they told me, should have been in Tollesbury swinging at one of their moorings, but had been for some months on the trots at Brightlingsea. A succession of would-be purchasers had been enquiring for her during the summer, but none of them had got anywhere. Mr Frost drew my attention to an old Cornish crabber, which was genuinely for sale, and lying right there in front of me. After due exchange of courtesies, I went on to Brightlingsea. It was October and the season was over; it was cold and blowy, and Brightlingsea was bleak and deserted. I borrowed a dinghy from the harbour-master and rowed over to the trots. *Privateer* was beginning to look a little forlorn. She had been lying here since the end of the summer, with no work being done on her and it was beginning to show. Of her two owners, one had got married and was about to become a father; they had to break up the partnership and sell, but their reluctance to take this final step had led to delays. Under a weather-beaten canvas cover, the cabin felt distinctly damp. A flock of seagulls had made their home on her afterdeck, and it looked as if there was a lot of green seaweed in their diet. Apart from these superficialities, *Privateer* gave a feeling of strength and stability. A traditional conver-sion, I supposed, she had the normal solid hull of an East Coast smack. Coming from Boston, she had more freeboard than the local smacks, and a more gentle entry. Thirty two feet overall, she had a beam of only nine feet. In a sea she would not behave exactly the same way as the smacks of the Blackwater; her fine bow would cut into the waves rather than hit down on them. On to this solid hull, of redwood pine on solid grown-oak frames, had been built a cabin high enough to give standing headroom under the skylight, with a doghouse aft which meant that you could step down below rather than climb in. The main cabin had ample length for two bunks, with a wide floor space between. Up forward was a pipecot and a rack for spare sails. Behind the bunks and under them, were lockers and drawers. There were more of these up in the fo'c'sle, while there was a capacious bo'suns locker aft of the cockpit and extending under the deck. The cockpit had more locker space under the seats, besides two large water tanks, one either side, and signs of a petrol engine under the cockpit floor. Under the doghouse was the galley on the port side and an oilskin locker on the starboard side. One of the things I like about a traditional boat is this generous allowance of storage space, and *Privateer* was not lacking in this respect.

Up on deck I braved the afternoon wind blowing up Brightlingsea Creek. The mast stood in a tabernacle, there seemed a lot of rigging all over the place and a long bowsprit pointed ahead close to the dolphin that she was tethered to. I knew that this was the boat I wanted.

Of course she was bigger than I could afford; and she would need a formidable amount of maintenance work done on her year after year. On the other hand, she would be a fine boat for cruising, and for introducing young children to the sea. Unlike our tiny catamaran, there was no possibility we would outgrow *Privateer* and once she was ours she would stay that way. Above all, she was undoubtedly a boat of character—we should not begrudge the labour we would have to put in to keep her seaworthy. I felt sure that she would prove to be a *rewarding* boat.

So, the next thing was to get her out of the water, have her surveyed, and start a negotiation with her owners.

A week or two later *Privateer* was on the hard at Brightlingsea, leaning up against the posts. Out of the water she looked enormous and for a moment my heart sank and I wondered if I could cope with such a lot of boat. Her bottom had the most awful growth on it; festoons of coral, an all-round fringe of green weed, and below it all a thick encrustation of barnacles. The surveyor was scratching away at various places, but could find nothing wrong below the waterline. Only in one place had a patch of rot on the decks spread below to her carline. This was the only blemish as far as the surveyor's report was concerned though he earned his fee with the usual remarks about fastenings and other such matters. *Privateer* needed quite a lot of routine work done on her, but very little else. Armed with the surveyor's report and an estimate for doing the work, I put in a bid.

In the purchase of a boat there's considerable leeway for pleasantness or unpleasantness. I have heard tales of owners advertising a boat as ready for sea, and then stripping her of everything that was not nailed down before handing over. Until you have to equip a boat you never realise what an enormous number of separate items have to come together to make her a going concern. Mr Pike and Mr Jarman—*Privateer*'s owners—were the opposite of this in their approach. First we got through the tricky business of negotiations, with much help from the East Coast Yacht agency. With a figure agreed, Mr Pike and Mr Jarman could not have been more helpful or friendly. They introduced me to the mysteries of the engine, then sixteen years old and awkward with it. They handed over the working manual, and wrote out their own version of instructions for starting. They made no bones about the fact that the sails had seen better days, and warned me that although there were three jibs, none of them was very good and I should need to think about a replacement before long. They explained to me how to turn a boat with a long keel to windward—something I had no experience of. They made over to me the entire inventory; navigation lamps, paraffin heater, scrubbers, mops, scrapers, paint brushes and long toms, paint pots, crockery, cutlery, mattresses, cushions, flags, spare warps—there was nothing missed out. All this left a good taste in the mouth.

In early January I went to the Boat Show, spoke to Mr East of the agency, and learned that the formalities had been completed and as from 1st January I was *Privateer*'s owner.

Privateer in 1966.

Out of the water in Frost & Drake's yard, Tollesbury.

CHAPTER II

Finding a Home

There was much to be done, and the first thing was to get *Privateer* into a yard and have the bit of rotten carline replaced. Something about Frost & Drake's yard in Tollesbury had appealed to me, and besides this was really *Privateer*'s home port and not Brightlingsea, so the first necessity was to bring her round to the Blackwater. Now this may not seem like a very momentous passage, but in order to get up Woodrolfe creek in Tollesbury, and then through the 'ditch' to Frost & Drake's slip, it seemed to me that I must have a working engine. The boat was strange to me, and besides she had a most effective braking system firmly attached to her hull. Nothing would persuade the engine to start, although I tried to follow the detailed instructions I had been given. One of my crew then was a doctor called Ken and he was accustomed to performing operations under difficult conditions; by lying on his back and working with his arms above his head he was able to reach the distributor head and adjust the points while I held a small vanity mirror so that he could see what he was doing. The operation was a complete success, and the patient coughed into life; it was February, and a very light breeze was blowing into Brightlingsea. We hoisted sail and made our way slowly and cautiously round to Frost & Drake's.

Work could now begin, and I was able to harness the

9

energies of three children—eight, ten and thirteen—to
the many tasks ahead. Cathy and Will worked their way
into the after locker and oilskin locker, paintbrush in
hand; Christopher, the eldest, helped me with a garden
hoe to separate ourselves from the barnacles. Mr Frost
meanwhile worked away at scarfing in a bit of oak in the
carline and, while he was at it, a new taffrail. We quickly
saw eye to eye about one thing; it was a waste of
Mr Frost's time (and my money) for him to clear up
shavings and replace the inner skin where it had to be
removed, so that such menial tasks were left for my
unskilled hands. This was the first but not the last time
that I established this division of labour with a skilled
shipwright. Mr Frost regaled us with stories about how
he caught flounders in the creek; at the right state of the
ebb he walked along the mud and caught them with his
hands. The crabs used to run up the sleeve of his coat
and he brushed them off when they reached the shoulder.
I had not come across this method of fishing before, but
Mr Frost could fill a bucket this way. At one time he
and Des Drake got the idea that I used Calor gas for
cooking. I did have a cylinder which I used for a burner
and there had been some conversational misunderstanding. Mr Frost and Mr Drake determined to make me
change what they thought were my evil ways, and they
did this by an antiphony of stories about Calor gas
fires and explosions. I remember the climax of these
stories in which an owner had retired to the fo'c'sle and
was sitting on the heads just below the forward hatch,
all unknowing that the Calor gas had been leaking down
below him. He decided to have a smoke, filled his pipe,
lit it and threw the match away without extinguishing it.
Des Drake described graphically how this peaceful pipe
smoker was blown out through the hatch; I suddenly

realised what he and John Frost were getting at, and spoilt the point of their story by blurting out that I would never use anything but paraffin.

While we were in the yard and up on the slip, it occurred to me it would be a good moment for one bit of work to be done. I asked Des to fit a transducer, so that later I could attach a Seafarer depth sounder to it. I explained that I had no money left for the Seafarer itself. At once Des brushed this objection aside, and offered to get me a complete Seafarer. I should pay for it when I could, but now was the time to have the use of it, before I got to know the river better. I had reason to be grateful to Des for this generosity, as my earlier method of using a 10 ft bamboo pole is less effective at keeping you off the ground. In due course I paid the £20 or so I owed, and this was one of the best bargains I ever had. On the East Coast the hazards all lurk invisibly below the surface and the Seafarer will give you advance warning that you are coming up to a shelf.

In those days there were two yards in Tollesbury, Frost & Drake, to which I adhered, and Drake Brothers, which was on the site of the present marina. One day, Des remarked reflectively what a pity it was about the quarrel, but something interrupted him and I never did learn what had started the rift in the Drake family.

By the Spring we were all fitted out and smartened up. I had found some incredibly cheap antifouling in Chelmsford and filled up a dozen gallon cans with it. It was to last for years, getting less and less effective all the while. At the same time I had bought a lot of old Admiralty grey paint, and this was the only colour we needed for the hull, the cabin and all the spars. Just about everything got painted that first year, including such places as the inside of the hull which was only to be reached by brushes with long wire handles that could be bent to pass over the top of the inner skin.

One of the matters that had to be settled was where we were to keep *Privateer*. Tollesbury had the advantage of being her home port, where she had lain for the past four years, but we had no special links with the place; it did have the disadvantage that there is no access until half tide, unless you leave your dinghy down a mile walk along the sea wall at the 'causeway'. West Mersea on the other hand was an all-states-of-the-tide anchorage, and I made some enquiries there at the two yards. The charges for a mooring seemed rather heavy, and there was also the problem of overcrowding; even with an engine that worked it would be quite difficult to manoeuvre to some of the buoys there. I also went over to Maylandsea and talked to Cardnells; instead of answering my question about the cost of a mooring, Mr Cardnell asked *me* some questions. 'Oh, yes we do all the laying up and fitting out, yes we have a go at caulking the decks' I prattled on. At the end of this, Mr Cardnell must have decided that I was not the sort of customer he was looking for. During our first year we were gradually succumbing to the discreet charm of Tollesbury, and finding that in practice the limitation over the tide trickling up Woodrolfe Creek was not such a drawback as we expected. However, something happened towards the end of the summer which took the matter out of our hands and settled it for good.

We had put ashore some weekend guests one afternoon, and my eldest boy, Chris, was rowing them up to the hard, leaving me on board with his younger brother Will, then eight years old. Will was messing about with the little pram we used for a tender, and which was quite a nice little boat to row on your own. Making the usual parental remark about not getting too far away, I had gone below to busy myself with one of the endless tasks of a gaffer owner. I thought I heard some noise from the seawall, and there was someone shouting and gesticulating; at first I couldn't see what they were concerned about, but downstream was a small dinghy, overturned and floating slowly out with the ebb. About half way towards it was Will, in the pram. I yelled to him to come back, but he took no notice and rowed on. When he came up with the capsized dinghy, he took its painter and made it fast to the ring in the stern transom, then pulled as hard as he could for the muddy shore. The man and woman in the dinghy had both stayed with their boat, and hung on now till Will had pulled them up onto the edge of the mudbank. By this time I arrived, having swum ashore on Cob Island and run along the mud. Will and I now got the dinghy the right way up, and took the survivors of the capsize aboard the nearest boat, the beautifully kept *Quickstep*, a fine 40-footer from the Solent which belonged to a wealthy local owner. One of the occupants of the dinghy was Ted Gager, then in his sixties; he had the lean shanks of an old man, and was suffering obviously from exposure. We got him aboard, wrapped him in blankets, put a hot drink on to boil and (my medical knowledge was very scant in those days) gave him some rum to drink. We were getting a lot of help from the other survivor, Pat Sisson who was a doctor. Younger than Ted, she was better covered and misleadingly athletic. She looked after herself while we rubbed Ted, who was in considerable distress for an hour or so before he dropped off to sleep. Ted and Pat had in fact been on their way to the *Quickstep* when their dinghy had capsized, due to using too much helm on the outboard engine. Ted was the paid hand on the *Quickstep*—I suppose he must have been one of the last paid hands in Tollesbury—and had come back the previous night from Ostend. He had been left there by the owner when a series of strong westerlies had prevented them coming home. At last the weather had changed, and Ted had enlisted a pierhead crew in Ostend to make the crossing. The crew turned out to be worse than useless, and Ted had brought the boat back on his own. He had arrived back on the one day that Mrs Gager, eagerly awaiting his return, had taken time off to visit relatives, so that when he got home there was no-one there. Hence the trip with Pat back in the dinghy, to sort out some duty frees and other stores that he had brought back from Belgium. Pat Sisson owned the little old gaffer, the *Star* and lived in a 15th century house opposite the Church. Her husband Guy was the agent for one of the companies that specialise in chartering barges.

By the time Ted and Pat were rested, it was low water and there was no hope of getting ashore until after ten o'clock at night. We had a sort of mobile party that began on *Quickstep,* moved to *Privateer* and finished up on the *Star.* Finally we set off for the village and arrived after the Kings Head had shut, collected Mrs Gager—after some explanations from me about what had happened—and finished up at the Sissons. Not for the last time I was getting the benefit of something that I had not done. I have heard of cases where people have been pulled out of the water and did not stop to say thank you to their rescuer; but Pat Sisson was the extreme opposite case. Years later, if I walked into the Kings Head she would hail me, remind everyone of the incident, and enquire after Will—perhaps by that time a graduate student and married, but in her eyes still her eight-year-old rescuer.

Ted also showed his gratitude in a very thoughtful and practical way; he gave an underwater gun to Chris, the elder brother who was feeling very left out indeed. This was one of the most tactful and sensitive things that anyone could have done. Ted was unhappy about the incident, and I felt for him; in my day too it was not done to capsize a boat, although every dinghy sailor nowadays is taught to do so. I haven't capsized a boat yet myself, although there is still time for me; my father was in a day boat that capsized when he was seventy-six and this was his first and last spill.

Soon after this incident Ted was paid off the *Quickstep*, the boat was sold, and he took up a new career as the Hardmaster at Tollesbury. The owners of speed boats and others wanting to launch went in awe of him.

After this incident, there was really no more question of where we should moor; I spoke to Des Drake and we stayed on our old mooring for the agreed sum of £9 per year.

Our first year we savoured the pleasures of ditch crawling for the first time in our own boat. We made trips to Pin Mill, where we used to search for mussels at low water, to Walton where we would picnic on the sand at Stone Point, to Shotley, where the weather always fulfilled my prediction and gave us a Shotley squall—icy cold and wet. I had done time in HMS *Ganges* and knew that the weather there was uniquely awful. We felt our way around the Blackwater, tacking up Maylandsea Creek, and we grounded coming in and out of Bradwell. We anchored off Osea and swam on the beach there. We went up to Heybridge Basin, but only to land and introduce my children to the Jolly Sailor. The lady behind the bar had served my father forty years previously and remembered him well. And of course we went to West Mersea, tacking down the narrow channel inside the Nass and dropping our anchor in Mersea quarters. We learnt much about *Privateer* that first year. We found that leaks in the deck would seek us out in the night and drip on our sleeping heads, and so we learned to patch the caulking. We tried pitch, marine glue, Bostik, Jeffreys, and Mastic. Still the rain found its way in. We learned where the best places were to careen, for my bargain antifouling only lasted a few weeks and soon

Familiar sight, careening for a scrub.

we had another crop of barnacles to dispose of. We found that Osea island was best for doing her port side, the shingle on Stone Point at East Mersea best for the starboard side; while the posts at Brightlingsea were fine if you wanted to clean up both sides at once without renewing the paint. We learned how to coax the engine into life; almost every start it needed to have the plugs cleaned, and this was something that others with all their skill could no more alter than I could. I learnt how to clean up the carburettor, almost always there was dirt and water in it. I learnt how to spin the starting motor so that it would engage. We found out how best to persuade *Privateer* round through the wind in a light air, and also when turning into the waves outside in the Wallet; when to back the staysail, and when to give up the idea of tacking into the wind altogether and gybe her round instead. We also spent an inordinate amount of time trying to keep our tender afloat. This was a pleasingly shaped clinker pram about eight feet long. We kept it ashore in between our sailing weekends and the sun would open it out so that daylight could be seen through the seams.

In October we declared our first season over, and put *Privateer* into a mud berth in the saltings just opposite Frost & Drake's slip. Down came the mast, we labelled all the running and standing rigging as we stored it away. There seemed rather a lot of it. A capacious heavy plastic cover—one of the uncovenanted items which came with the boat—went over her and we settled down to the Tollesbury winter.

CHAPTER III

Beginnings

In this account of our early days with *Privateer,* I have said nothing about one sequel to becoming her new owner. In due course the Certificate of Registry arrived and so I opened out the folded linen sheet of this ancient-looking document and scanned the details. *Privateer* had been registered in 1935, a few years after she was built; the name of the second owner caught my eye:

The Certificate of Registry is a fine traditional document, unfortunately too large to reproduce here. A list of the owners is to be found on p 193.

William Whitworth, Headmaster of Framlingham College. The laconic entry, in the Maldon Customs Officer's best copperplate handwriting, took me back to my childhood.

My father, a Maldon man, had come to Orford after the First World War to manage the oysterage at Butley Creek, with the help of Charlie Stoker, who brought his smack up from West Mersea. My father sold his yacht the *Uldra* and had a five-tonner, the *Hind* built at Harland & Wolfs. She arrived about the same time as I did, and I can remember fighting for possession of the helm with my sister when I was about four. Before that we would both sit in the stern sheets of the dinghy where father had taken out the after thwart, the better to control us with his feet, as he explained. Every morning after my 'schooling', conducted by my mother who trusted no-one else with this job, I would run down to the quay and along the seawall to the hard, where I would raise my treble voice to hail '*Hind* Ahoy'. Father would row over to collect me and I would leap aboard, have a spoonful of condensed milk, and settle down to the job of Ship's Boy. Father would teach me how to make up a grommet, how to tie a bowline with one hand, and how to make up a Swedish coil of the main sheet. Then we would sail up and down the river, with much beating to windward, as the wind on the Ore is almost always up and down. When we were not painting or tanning the sails or sailing, father would be yarning away and I would be soaking up the wisdom of a very experienced sailor. These were the days of father's old age, when he rarely sailed beyond the mouth of the river, but he had been a notable sailor in his time, and had sailed the *Joli Brise* with George Martin, raced on the Blackwater and cruised from Brest to the Baltic in *Uldra*. His racing days were over, but he used to start the races for the local Dabchicks every Saturday and I can still hear his voice calling through the megaphone 'Five minutes gun in one minute's time!' and see his stopwatch which he held in his left hand while he kept a weather eye on the starting line to see that no-one was across when Bomber Lewis fired the gun. When I was six I went on the only 'cruise' with my father—we sailed down the Gulls and up Butley Creek, where I climbed into one of the woollen sleeping bags while we spent the night at anchor. I learnt how to sail the *Hind,* which was a handy gaff sloop, and from an early snapshot it looks as if I were sailing her single-handed. I can have been only seven when this photo was taken, as that was the year of the Slump, and father was compelled to sell the *Hind* for what he could get. That was the end of 'cruising', but we were soon sailing in a 13-foot lugsail dinghy, the *Sylvia.* She was too slow and heavy to race, even in those days, but made an excellent boat for me to learn in. So, we sailed the *Sylvia* up and down the river, dickering about among the shoals at the Mouth, and trailed a spinner where the tide ran fast over the shingle. Never once did a tunny-fish or any other fish take our hook, but the line and the long bamboo pole were always rigged astern.

Although *Sylvia* was no racing boat, father did not neglect this aspect of my education, and apprenticed me to George Weyman, an ex-Chief Petty Officer who sailed the *Isis,* one of the old gaff-rigged 14-footers. Every Saturday we used to race and when it blew hard, the *Isis* could do well against the Marconi rigged boats and be first across the line. Later I graduated to being crew for Margaret Tudor who sailed one of the new National Twelves. Here I had to learn to be much faster with the jib sheet than with the heavily built *Isis*. When it came to the under-fourteen's race, I think it was *Isis'* helm that I took.

After five years of dinghy sailing, father began to yearn for a yacht again. He was now over seventy, and was thinking of something small and modest. Looking over the boats at Ipswich one day he saw the *Siwash* up for sale. Forty years previously he had had her built, at Howards in Maldon—his first boat, not counting dinghies. She was twenty feet long, half decked and gunter rigged with a centre board and a lot of ballast, inside and outside. His first boat, she was also to be his last, as he bought her back and fitted her with a cabin-top. We sailed her together until father was eighty-four.

Father had been one of the founder members of the Royal Cruising Club, and it was perhaps because of that that anyone who sailed up the river would come to visit, have a bath, maybe a meal and a bed for the night and certainly to talk boat. In those days the Mouth was worse than it is now—there was rarely more than three feet at low water and the position of the channel was apt to change faster than the leading marks could be moved. Not many yachtsmen would attempt the passage to Orford, and nearly all of them would do so only with the help of one of the pilots. There were two of these at Shinglestreet, and they had to be ready to bring in yachtsmen and also the regular Thames barges that came up to Snape Maltings.

In spite of these difficulties, there was a regular procession of yachtsmen who came up river every summer, almost all of whom would find their way to our house. I have a child's hazy recollections of some of them, others stand out in my memory. I remember Professor Gardiner who brought his barge yacht the *Chequers* up to Orford every summer with his family aboard. He was a marine biologist from Cambridge and was on the trail of some rare worm. Professor Gardiner had the rather unexpected ambition of running the fishmongers in the middle of Cambridge. I remember being allowed to take the wheel of *Chequers,* a new experience for me and actually much easier to handle for a child than a tiller. Another boat I remember well was the *Moonraker,* there was something very special about her, although in those days she had not sailed to Alaska and become famous.

And I remember Mr Whitworth. At that time in my life I was terrified of headmasters, but there was nothing intimidating about him. A source of fascination to us children was that he had a wooden leg; had he lost it in the war, or through some accident? We never knew. There was another reason to remember him kindly; in return no doubt for the hospitality he had received, he invited me aboard his yacht for the night. This was a great treat, as I had only had one night aboard father's *Hind* before she was sold. How was it that I didn't remember that this was *Privateer?* I can only plead that in those days almost all the boats that came up the river were gaff cutters and there was nothing especially remarkable about her. All the same, it was a happy coincidence that I had known her and her owner all those years ago and that she was no stranger but an old friend.

Postscript
Since writing this chapter I have learned more about Mr Whitworth and the reason why be bought *Privateer*. In 1934 he had lost his previous yacht, the *Emba* in a collision in bad weather off the North Foreland. Before that he had lost the *Alektor* in 1924. He had written up both disasters in *Yachting Monthly* and they are reprinted in *Total Loss* by Jack Coote.

CHAPTER IV

Neighbours

Now that we had established ourselves on a mooring in Tollesbury Fleet, it did seem an entirely appropriate place for us to be—a natural habitat for old gaffers.

Not so long ago there were fifty or sixty working smacks there, crowding into Woodrolfe Creek to deliver their catch. Some would sit against each other on the hard, with legs lashed to the chain plates, unloading their catch to carts that came right down alongside. This was especially popular with the loads of five-fingers, or star-fish, which were collected by local farmers and used as manure. Others would huddle up to the saltings at Rickers, where a causeway had been built to take the hand-carts. At the head of the creek the fishermen had put up the drying sheds, the summit of their great co-operative effort in the early 1900s. Here were the two yards, Frost & Drake, and Drake Brothers, where smacks were built and were still being repaired. In other words, Tollesbury was just the place to attract Old Gaffers; and attract them it did.

No doubt about where to begin; with the *Boadicea*, one of the most famous boats on our coast and easily the oldest gaffer afloat. The details of her story have appeared in more than one book, told by her present owner, Mike Frost, who has been her custodian since 1938. When we first came to Tollesbury, the *Boadicea* had been put up on a cradle in Frost & Drake's, and every weekend as we came down for our sailing we followed the progress as she was rebuilt. Originally built in 1808, Mike had found her in West Mersea where she had fallen on evil days and lay out of commission. He had put her on the slip to replace a bit of keel that had gone, but one thing had led to another, and he was eventually to replace keel, ribs and planks. As soon as he realised what needed doing, Mike bought an oak tree; this lay by the sea-wall cut into slices two inches thick and weathering. For the frames he used to visit a timber yard in Earls Colne and pick out a suitable branch of oak. The next week he would fit this, then the cycle would start again with looking for another branch with the right curve in it. In all it took ten years of intensive work to rebuild the *Boadicea,* and one memorable day she was launched down the slip and took her place at the mooring next to ours. For some years we enjoyed Mike's company, until one day he fitted the old *Boadicea* with an engine, which perhaps made it possible for him to keep her a bit nearer home. Anyway, one dark December night when we were lying on our mooring and sitting by our stove, *Boadicea* came up the Fleet, picked up her mooring anchors one after the other, and carried them off to her new berth in Mersea quarters.

Tollesbury has remained a place for smacks, and when we first moved in there were two fine conversions, Bill Quill's *Phantom* and Walter Bibby's *Taffy.* Both have long gone, but many others have followed them, perhaps to slip in Frost & Drake's yard, or to work away in the saltings.

Another near neighbour was the delightful little gaff cutter *Rose of Paglesham;* like *Boadicea,* her owner was a dentist. (Perhaps there are similarities between dealing with patches of rot on an old wooden boat and filling teeth?). Kit now has a new gaffer, the *Miranda*, and is apt to carry away cups with her. But the old *Rose* is still on the end of our line of moorings.

Also in that line is the *Deva*, a yacht built on More-cambe Bay Prawner lines; whether due to Jon Wainwright's skill or to her design or to a combination of both, the *Deva* has established a justified reputation as a winner of races—and not only against other gaffers. Jon arrived in Tollesbury after a somewhat unusual voyage which started through a sort of oversized drain in Liverpool and wound its way through the disused locks across and over the Pennines.

For many years our next door neighbour has been a fine classic yacht, the *Fearnought*, built in 1898, and owned since 1970 by Mike Gibson. Unfortunately, she was converted to Bermuda rig by some smart Alec in the 1930s, and my efforts to persuade Mike to convert her back to gaff have not so far proved successful.

Further down the Fleet lies the *Charlotte Ellen* a fine old smack done up with loving care by John Rigby. He had spent years working on her and soon after the work was finished, she suffered a tragic and near fatal accident. Beating through the Maplin channel one October night, she took the ground on a falling tide. As the tide receded, she sewed into the sand and when the tide began to flood, the waves beating against her shook her timbers and loosened the caulking. Soon she was full of water and sand and had to be abandoned. Undaunted by this, John quickly got together a team to refloat her, and with the aid of airbags she was given enough buoyancy to tow her back into Tollesbury. Once again she was taken ashore and worked on, and she is now afloat again and challenging the leading smacks in the

East Coast Race. (Before the last one I noticed her up on the posts and taking off her prop.)

Up Woodrolfe Creek lies a little gaff yacht, the *Greenshank*, with an unusual canoe stern. *Greenshank* had her moment of glory when she suddenly appeared at the head of the Old Gaffers race in the Ijsselmeer. Further still up the creek lies the *Olga*, a Bristol Pilot Cutter, built in 1906. The owner, Roger Robinson, who sailed to Rio once with Tilman, has been working on her and has replaced a number of planks and the whole of the deck. I fear that when he has finished work on her he will sail her off somewhere where there is more water for a boat that draws nine feet.

At one time the *Luna* (ex *Meridian*) a converted Baltic ketch used to lie in Tollesbury, where her owners worked on fitting out her cabins for chartering; but she also has sailed away to deeper waters. In her place lies an old Maldon smack, the *Ripple,* which used to belong to Sadds.

In our early days we used to lie for the winter in the saltings, not far from the old wooden sheds. Here we would do our fitting out every spring as soon as the weather was right for it, and watch all the other boats fitting out as well. One day I remember a boat that was rather far gone, and the owner was clearly in that state of mind which is balancing between varnishing the tiller and setting fire to some shavings. In his case, he had first decided to varnish his for'ard hatch. But, changing his mind, the next moment we heard an explosion and he had thrown on a can full of petrol. At the second attempt the boat burned right away and left only the rusty remains of an engine, still there in the rill. Another time I was fitting out with the help of Roy Barber, who had sold his own boat, a gaff yawl called the *Abaca,* and also of the Mulville boys, whose father Frank was away for a single-handed voyage to Cuba. Paddy Mulville had decided that there was a ford across the neck of Woodrolfe creek, but in fact there is nothing but very soft mud, and he was soon stuck fast. Roy and I hastened to his aid and propelled a dinghy over the mud alongside Paddy; I grasped him firmly round the waist and pulled; nothing happened. Roy, who is large, then grasped me firmly round the waist and *he* pulled. Paddy came out of the mud with a popping sound, and something went snap under my pullover. Later the doctor said it was probably a broken rib, but there was no point in diagnosis as nothing could be done except let it heal, which it did.

Whenever we can we sail up and down Woodrolfe Creek, but it is not wide and is lined now with a row of fishing boats and others moored either side all the way up; so we cannot sail it without a fair breeze. Many is the

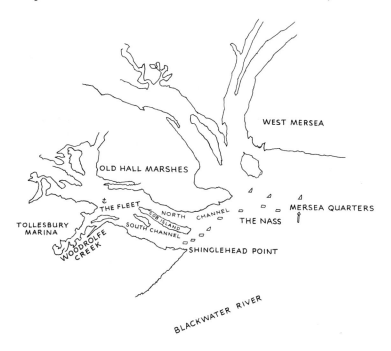

time we have come up under oars, that is towing with the dinghy. Sweeps would be better but ours were lost long ago and I haven't replaced them. Rowing may be slower, but is safer than coming up under power, even when we have the option and the engine will start. It is, to say the least, difficult to stop her way when coming up by engine, whereas when towing with dinghy you can pull her up hard and turn her in her own length. Often we have come up the creek specifically to try to get the engine mended, and several skilled mechanics have tried their hand at our Vedette.

Old Will Drake's yard has in the intervening years become a marina, and I have once or twice ventured in, to swing an engine out or mend a skin fitting. But I notice that whereas, down the Fleet there congregate all the old wooden boats, in the marina there are ten times the number of modern yachts; boats of a feather, it seems, like to keep each others' company.

Until the marina was built there were no scrubbing posts at Tollesbury, at least not in my time, but there is an amenity which for us was as good or perhaps even better. Down the Fleet and past Shinglehead, Tollesbury creek winds, a narrow channel between the Cob Islands on one side and the great mile long spit known as the Nass, on the seaward side. A cable or so down this spit is a small horse of shells, standing up three or four feet above the hard mud of the Nass, and with a steep shelving edge into the channel. Here is a splendid place to scrub off and paint; clean, protected from all winds, and with good holding ground in the bottom of the creek when it comes to heaving off. On a warm summer day it's a lovely spot for a bathe, and we have often shared an afternoon with a party of seascouts or lads from West Mersea.

I suppose we get to know our underwater hull fairly well, every scar and bruise and every seam and plank; each side gets, say, an average of four scrubs a year, that means around eight careenings every year. Recently I noticed a water pump with pressure hose being used to scrub off, at Brightlingsea. A conversion kit for the outboard? If only...

The marina has brought us two benefits, one unexpected. The buoyage for Tollesbury creek is now far better than it used to be, in fact there was a time when the buoys, like those in West Mersea, only appeared in summer, as to say that no-one should put to sea when there was no white cover on their yachting cap. This is a great amenity, and if you are beating up this narrow creek, it is hard enough not to go aground even when it is well marked by withies. The other benefit was more unpredictable, or at least unpredicted; the emptying of the large volume of water in the scooped-out bowl of the marina continues long after half tide, and has therefore scoured out the bottom of the creek. Whereas previously this dried just after half tide, there is now a narrow channel down the middle, exactly the width of our dinghy, and it is possible to push, shove and coax the dinghy down Woodrolfe at the bottom of the ebb. As against this, the spit at the entrance to Woodrolfe, known as the Whale has silted up with this scour, and we now have less water at our mooring than we did years ago.

This reminds me of something for which Tollesbury is notorious: gribble. With a keel that takes the mud every spring ebb, there is bound to be a danger of this, but I have only had one bad attack. I hope that by keeping her covered in anti-fouling I will discourage this evil worm. And I also make a point of staying two or three weeks each winter in Heybridge basin on the assumption that fresh water will do it no good. The year that I did find the tell-tale gribble holes in *Privateer*'s keel, I put her on the slip at Dan Webb and Feesey's, and she sat there for quite a while, with me squirting in varieties of poison through every opening. One day as I came up on *Privateer* she greeted me with a foul odour under her keel, and as soon as I realised what was causing it I celebrated victory over the enemy. Drying out is a fairly simple—though also costly— remedy; but before I tried it I had asked the experts, in this case Arthur Holt at the yard in Heybridge Basin. When I asked him what I should do about gribble, he replied without hesitation; 'try singing out of key'.

Unlike fashionable West Mersea across the mudflats, Tollesbury slumbered away, a quiet fishing village which has lost its fishing fleet. The attempt to give Tollesbury a deep water pier with its railway link at the beginning of the century has come and gone, and did not bring the expected prosperity.

Earlier in the last century the great Isambard Kingdom Brunel had been summoned to Tollesbury, according to his biographer to install a huge steam pumping engine. I often wondered what had become of this scheme, but have been enlightened by Mike Gibson. Apparently, what Brunel built was a syphon to drain the marshes, and this was still working within a long living memory. When first installed, the syphon failed to work until it was discovered that one of the valves had been put in the wrong way round.

In my father's log book for 1912, I see that Tollesbury used to have a regatta, but this tradition has lapsed. I have a feeling that the very active Sailing Club and the Cruising Club based on the marina may one day remedy this.

CHAPTER V

Race

It's the last Saturday in July; just above Stone is an extraordinary sight—scores and scores of Old Gaffers, tacking in and out, luffing and gybing, backing headsails and letting go sheets—getting ready for the event of the year, the East Coast Old Gaffers Race. Like the population of China, nobody ever knows exactly how many there are; eighty or ninety boats send in the entry form, about the same number take part and finish. Bad weather one year may prevent the Medway gaffers from getting over in time; no wind at all often causes a few to give up and go home. But you can be sure that there will be a large turn-out every year and that they will provide one of the finest sights to be seen anywhere.

The East Coast gaffers race had started a year or two previously, and we had watched as spectators; now we had our first opportunity to take part ourselves.

Our first year, soon after the start, there was a fracas ahead, and sadly *Fanny of Cowes* was quite badly damaged; coming out of the melée and out of control a gaffer came straight at us, her bowsprit narrowly missing Roy Barber who was sitting in the scuppers and scraping over the doghouse, where the slope acted as a brake. We disentangled with only the loss of the dog-house handrail, which I replaced some twelve years later. After that first year we did not crowd the starting line, and resigned ourselves to the fact that *Privateer* is not a fast boat. With so many entrants, there is always someone to race against, in our case it is often the Tollesbury smack *William and Emily,* universally known as the *Odd Times,* and built in Drake Brothers yard a hundred years ago. Year after year at some point in the race we will find ourselves sailing cranch iron to cranch iron with the *Odd Times,* exchanging friendly insults or trimming sheets to try to edge ahead.

But the Old Gaffers race is craftily designed; as we beat slowly up from the North Buxey to the Wallet Spit, we see the leaders with all their topsails, flying jibs, jury spinnakers and water sails coming down across our bows to the Bench Head. No need to be in the steam tug *Brent* which keeps us company up and down the river to get a good view of the race or at least of the old gaffers in it. We can hear about the finish at the bar afterwards.

What a sight these boats are; up in front are the big smacks and bawleys. The *Hyacinth, Peace, ADC, Dorothy, Stormy Petrel,* a whole flotilla of smacks from West Mersea. Here there is a special tradition of racing and in the days of the working smacks they were all keenly raced; many of these have been restored and given a wardrobe of sails to get the most out of them. There are now smack races in the Blackwater, the Colne and across the estuary on the Swin. The Tollesbury men also have a tradition of racing of a different sort; it was from here that many of the crews were recruited for the pre-1914 racing yachts. I must not forget that it is not only smacks up in front, there are fine old yachts like *Providence* owned by John Morrison, who used to sail Maurice Griffiths' old boat the *Nightfall.* To my surprise the old Deben Cherubs, which as a child I never thought of as being racers, do very well, in particular *Sea Pig,* sailed by

Tom and Wendy. Many of the smaller boats end up along
with the bawleys or even ahead of them, like *Mayhi,* a
pre-war One-design. One of the most unlikely winners is
the *Sheena;* pulled out of the mud as a near derelict and
done up by a very young man from Maldon called

Frank would keep standing on the spinnaker boom.

'Pudding', she had the misfortune to sink the day before
the race. Pudding and his friends pumped her out,
entered the race, and flying a variety of old sails poking
out at all angles, beat the whole field and were first
across the line.

Not only the old boats feature despite the 'O' in O.G. From Heybridge Basin comes the Arthur Holt-built *Martha Kathleen,* a fine wooden ketch, and the *Skua,* surely the most sightly concrete boat ever built. Made by her owner, Mick, she is built on Colin Archer lines, modified slightly to make the concrete construction possible. One or two Dutch barges in the area, like the *Saskia van Rijn* add a picturesque touch, though they cannot expect to do well against boats with more keel. Some larger boats take part, like the two Baltic trading ketches, the *Luna* and the *Solvig,* tragically lost in the Mediterranean.

For some reason, the last weekend in July nearly always turns out to be a day for a drifting-match; and *Privateer,* with her very snug rig, almost a cut-down mainsail really and no topsail, is never going to keep up with more heavily canvassed boats. The one year that it blew a gale, we were stuck round in the Orwell, perhaps it was just as well as I think only five boats finished the course that day, and we saw a barge dismasted as we clung to our mooring below Pin Mill. But this doesn't discourage us from taking part, and we try to get back in time from our holiday every year if we can; twice we have been too late for the start but have come in and watched the race from the unusual angle of being ahead of it. The only year we did comparatively well there was a miracle. We had made a particularly bad start and were well behind the fleet, which all got to the Bench Head long before us, where they found it impossible to stem the tide. When we arrived, with a ghost of a breeze astern, at the turning mark, the whole fleet was at anchor spread out below the buoy. At that moment the miracle occurred, and the wind suddenly turned and blew from the seaward; before the faster boats could pass us we took advantage of the occasion to photograph them through the gallows, *astern* of us.

Lastly, though not necessarily at the tail end, are the 'Class 3' or very small boats, whalers, Scottish fishing

3. This snap shows us ahead of   We are soon overtaken again;
    the fleet in the East Coast Old   the foreground the Baltic ketch
    Gaffers Race.   *Solvig.*

skiffs like the *Annie Laurie,* cutters like the *Golden Plover,* and barge boats like the *Buttercup.* If the last twenty years have seen a considerable movement to rescue old gaffers and restore them, the last year or two has seen a move to restore these old barge boats and dinghies, and these are now being raced keenly at Tollesbury.

Perhaps because I cannot hope to race *Privateer* successfully, I tend to treat what others take more seriously as a race, as an enjoyable rally; so that we bring aboard as many as possible to share our pleasure. Aside from my regular crews, we take aboard whole families, not always folk who are accustomed to sailing. One year our English crew were outnumbered by a French contingent (Will has married a French girl) whose Gallic wit was not always appreciated by some of the more staid old gaffers. That year we were given the Cup for Trying, and felt we deserved it. Another time we had a load of French children who spoke no English, and all the orders had to be repeated bi-lingually. At the other extreme we had an old veteran of square rig ships aboard, Frank Brookesmith. He would keep standing on the spinnaker boom, the nearest equivalent I suppose to a yard that he could find. This worried me as our spinnaker boom, so-called, is only a flimsy old tent-pole, and Frank

An exciting moment in the East Coast Race, as a stern-wind brings us all together to round the Inner Bench Head.

was nearly eighty at the time. One year, due to a misunderstanding about the rendezvous and other mis-
fortunes, I started the race entirely on my own. There
was virtually no wind, and this was one of the occasions
when the engine refused to start, so the race was started
close in to the shore at Stone where I had been hoping to
pick up my emergency crew. They arrived after the start
and scrambled aboard from a dinghy just before we were
swept on the shoal round the corner in St Lawrence bay.
My new crew were not at all put out by this, most of
them got out their buckets and spades and started to
look for crabs, while the grown-ups among us enjoyed a
rare view of the finish of the race.

Our first race we finished last; future performances
could only be an improvement. But already we were
planning to miss the next year's race; we had set our
sights on further horizons.

This race has continued into the evening—evidently a drifting
match.

CHAPTER VI

Going Foreign

Our first year we had been getting used to *Privateer* and her ways in the waters we knew best; the Blackwater, Colne, Stour and Orwell. As we fitted out for our second year, our thoughts were reaching out beyond the East Coast rivers. With such a stable and seaworthy boat nothing would stop us going foreign as soon as we could. For this first cruise abroad, my two boys, Chris now fifteen and William now nine, formed a reliable and experienced crew. Somewhere I had heard that Honfleur was a nice harbour to go to, so we started our voyage 'Towards Honfleur' as the old masters of sailing ships used to phrase it. We had rashly made a rendezvous there for the 1st August, but that gave us exactly a week from Dover, which did not seem excessive. I had equipped myself with an ancient chart from Ramsgate to Boulogne, a brand new Admiralty chart from there to Cap d'Antifer, and a small chart of the entrance to the Seine. At the last minute I added a copy of the Admiralty *Channel Pilot* which impressed me with its authority and solidity. So, stocked up with tins, reassured by a favourable weather forecast, and pleased to be leaving our anchorage in Dover outer harbour where we had been rolling too much for comfort, we left the protection of the harbour wall and set course for the invisible coast on the far side.

Nothing is quite like that first leap into the unknown; even though the crossing from Dover is the shortest possible way across the Channel, there was still something special about crossing from the island to the continent. It took a long time for people to treat that crossing as routine. Even in late Roman times they still thought Britain was a mist-shrouded island of ghosts, and when Caesar came to invade us he made no allowance for tides and came near to disaster. We had the advantage of tide tables and laid off a course for Gris Nez

As soon as we were clear of the land a fine westerly breeze came up and we were soon making good five knots or so over a moderate cross sea. But with Dover cliffs only a couple of miles astern we then ran into a thick mist, or rather a fog bank with some fairly dense patches. Every time we came out of a thick patch we had a good look around and made a note of the course and speed of any ships we could see. The channel in those days, before the shipping lanes were introduced, was very much of a free-for-all. We could hear the foghorn on the Varne Lightship getting louder all the time, and soon we were charging through the Varne bank overfalls. It was quite rough here with the wind against tide, but we came through fairly dry. A swirl in the fog showed the Light-ship very close and confirmed our course for Gris Nez. From then on we heard the engines of one or two big ships but saw nothing at all. Another rough patch we decided must be the Colbert bank. After this the fog patches began to give way to clearer weather, and we were relieved to see the French headland more or less where it was supposed to be on the port bow. We passed Gris Nez four-and-a-half hours out from Dover and set course down the coast to Boulogne. The wind now began to fall away, while the tide decided it had helped us enough already and began to set up the coast against us. We made a very slow reach up to the harbour entrance and at last crept into the outer harbour. I could see that, unlike Dover, no-one anchored in the outer harbour here, so I pulled up out of the fairway and downed sails. A French yachtsman seeing us hovering uncertainly assured us that we could sail straight in to the inner harbour without bothering ourselves with the highly complicated traffic lights, so we motored gently up to the pontoons at the head of the inner harbour and made fast. We had made our first passage.

French harbours are not adapted to *Privateer*. In the East Coast harbours that we were accustomed to we could sail up, find a bit of space out of the fairway and drop our anchor. Mersea Quarters, Brightlingsea, Pyefleet, Pin Mill, Walton Backwaters—none of these presented any problem. In Boulogne we came up against the difficulties of manoeuvring in a restricted space. Our long bowsprit, preceding us by a full four metres, had already caused a few anxious faces to appear through hatchways as it approached; there are inherent difficulties in getting a heavy boat with a long straight keel to turn round, but there were further difficulties which the spectators may not have understood. The first was that our engine simply would not work going astern. We had tried everything, all the experts had tried, but the best that could be achieved was to get the propeller turning very slowly astern—not fast enough to make stern way or even to check her forward way very noticeably; if I then tried to open the throttle the clutch slipped and some evil smelling smoke poured out of the gear case, but no sternway resulted. There was another bad habit that the engine had which was also it seemed incurable; it would idle forward when it was supposed to be in neutral. (The only real advantage of reverse gear was that it did stop the forward idling.) So coming in to the pontoons at Boulogne required space, patience and a lot of dinghy work and warping in. Warping usually proved the most satisfactory—if not the only—way of manoeuvring in harbour, but it is surprising how often people fail to understand what is going on and want to ride over the warp.

Any difficulties we had in no wise reduced our sense of triumph at berthing in our first foreign port. We sat in

Our long bowsprit preceded us by a full four metres.

the cockpit, watched the bubbles coming up from the bottom of the harbour, and the fishing boats discharging their catches on the quay opposite, and turned in early ready to move out the next morning.

Our next hop had to be a long one, across the Somme estuary to Dieppe. I had consulted the *Channel Pilot* and it was even more alarmist than usual about the Somme:

> 'The outer banks are composed of very fine shifting sand and constitute a formidable danger to vessels which ground on them, as the tidal streams tend to wash away the sand from under the extremities of such a vessel, causing her to break her back or capsize.'

Despite the restraint and the old-fashioned Navy jargon, that was a bit off-putting, and I have never ventured into the Somme estuary to see if it is exaggerated or not. An early start gave us the benefit of the ebb tide setting down the coast, and a South westerly breeze allowed us to fetch closehauled past the beach with the sand yachts racing at extraordinary speeds, and over the spit that marks the entrance to the Authie river, where we were sounding twelve feet and wondering if we should make a board to seaward.

The weather was clear and we soon picked up the Ault Lighthouse and other landmarks the other side of the Somme estuary; we made the best course we could with the wind falling away. So long as the tide was ebbing we were making progress, but as darkness fell the tide turned and we were beginning to get swept back the wrong way. Tough and dependable as my crew were, I did not think it reasonable to expect them to keep a night watch and so I had got them both tucked up in their bunks by 2200.

There was now about ten or twelve fathoms under us as we drifted over the outlying banks off the Somme, and the thought occurred to me that if I dropped the anchor I could get a bit of rest myself and at least we would be holding our own. On the East coast this was the normal procedure, if you ran out of tide coming down the Wallet, say. Accordingly I bent our longest warp on to the kedge and let it go, rolled up the jib and dropped the foresail and main with a rough stow.

Privateer was immediately all over the place; she rolled like anything, then she yawed around on her long scope and started to pitch. There was no question of going below for a nap, I sat miserably in the cockpit and tried to get her to lie more comfortably. Of course the wind had got up a bit as soon as the sails were down, and in fact began to blow from the landward now; *Privateer* contrived to get her stern towards the steep wavelets and slapped her counter down on them. Flying spray was added to my discomforts. This was too much, and I hoisted sail and raised the anchor from the depths; at once *Privateer* was her comfortable old self again, and this time we began to move in the right direction over the ground.

During the morning we made slow progress with the tide helping us along the coast, but it wasn't until late afternoon that we edged our way into Dieppe and made for the inner harbour. In the yacht club we saw *Privateer*'s name on the blackboard, and supposed the coast guards had been wondering what we had been up to since leaving Boulogne a day-and-a-half previously.

Dieppe was a good place to give ourselves a day off, and also to try to caulk the pram tender which had opened up again. It looked very good sitting bottom-up on the pontoon with a fresh coat of black varnish, which soon dried in the Continental sunshine.

After Dieppe there are no long hops, with the harbours spaced out at regular intervals along the Normandy coast. But with virtually no wind we had the same problem as before. First we drifted westwards with the tide, then when we tried to anchor we found we were too far out and had to edge our way in again until we were in ten or twelve fathoms. We lay like this until the evening, but not wanting to repeat our discomforts on the banks outside the Somme, we hoisted sail and ghosted gently into the night.

This night was not going to be peaceful either; ahead of us we saw the lights of a steamer—actually the Newhaven packet boat—approaching from ahead. When the side lights became visible they were an uncomfortable sight; red and green together, both showing. We watched for a bit as with the slight yawing first one light was eclipsed, then the other; then both were showing again. We tried shining a torch; evidently these people had not spotted our navigation lights. The torch made no impression, and the steamer came on relentlessly, and rather fast too. By this time the crew had been roused, and Chris set off a white flare. The packet boat was about a couple of cables off, and the whole scene was lit up as if someone had turned on the electric light. Before the flare died we had a searchlight trained on us while the steamer circled us slowly before hauling off on its way. It was our first encounter with a ship and it revealed to me something that I should have been aware of.

On one hand, since my earliest childhood I had a long experience of sailing, with every sort of sailing boat; and recently I had done a lot of ditch crawling around the East Coast, in charter boats and in *Privateer*. On the other hand I had spent some years of my life being trained as a navigator and steaming around in a destroyer, taking endless fixes and laying off tide triangles. Between these two areas of knowledge lay a gap in experience of what I was actually doing, that is cruising a small yacht in channel waters. When I had last been in these waters there would have been no call for any craft to have a radar reflector. Several pairs of eyes on every vessel afloat would be searching the horizon for a tiny point of light, a dark shape or a shimmer of wake as if their lives depended on it. These days, I now realised, no-one keeps a proper visual lookout, but most ships do keep an eye on their radar scan, where a yacht equipped with a reflector will show up at about four miles range. I also realised that our port and starboard paraffin lamps were fine-looking antiques but could not be seen at any range to speak of even by a ship that was keeping a lookout. I was to learn many other such lessons over the years.

There was hardly a breath of wind that night, so we drifted up and down with the tide. In daylight hours we anchored when the tide was foul, a slow but sure method of making progress up or down any coast. On the afternoon of the second day a warm front came over with some fairly heavy rain, which was coming straight down and blotting out the land. When it cleared we saw that we were off a small port. I had been intent on reaching Fécamp—a modest goal, at that—and had not noticed the existence of the little port of St-Valery-en-Caux. We hauled up the anchor and motored in. It had taken us five days to get here from Boulogne, and time was beginning to run out on us. I had to lose half my crew here; Chris had a rendezvous in Paris and this was the last possible day for him to catch the train. From here onwards my only crew was the nine-year-old Will, but he had enthusiasm and experience above his years.

We gave ourselves a rest at St Valery, an attractive little port with a lock leading to a spacious inner harbour. *Privateer* seems most at home in places like this which are half pleasure and half commercial.

At last our luck seemed to be on the turn, and the next day we had a fine breeze up our stern which took us right up to Cap d'Antifer, and we began to think we would really make Honfleur. Once again the wind dropped and we drifted down the coast towards Cap la Hève. Determined to save our tide we started up the engine and chugged on until we could see round the corner. There was the other bank of the Seine, with the buoyed channel full of ships going in and out, and there was the training wall, or dique, marked by beacons and showing at low water. In between us and the channel were the sands and shallows, with the water a most peculiar brown colour that I have never seen anywhere else. I cut the engine, which was beginning to get a bit hot and bothered, and we ghosted across the sands, not worried too much by the shallows as we were now on a rising tide and being swept into the estuary by the young flood. Soon we were in the narrow channel, seized our chance and crossed to the southern side of it and kept our hand on the banisters while the coasters and bigger ships came past and gave us the benefit of their wakes. We could see the town of Honfleur, but there was no sign of an entrance. Then a small sailing dinghy appeared out of the solid wall about half a mile ahead of us; now we could see the various landmarks, and we continued unhurriedly, with enough wind to give us steerage way. By the time we got to the opening the flood was giving us enough water to make our sharp turn to starboard and sail right up to the harbour entrance, up the narrow cut were the Newfoundland schooners and the great three-masters used to warp their way in, using a huge capstan which still stood by the lock gate.

The sailing barge *Margery,* when owned by the re-doubtable 'Pip' Pipe, once sailed up this narrow gut, and seeing the bridge opening as she came up to it, luffed through and into the inner harbour; she must have had several inches clearance either side. *Privateer* entered harbour less dramatically; we sat outside and waited till high water, then motored in using the last pint of our petrol.

Honfleur was every bit as wonderful a harbour as we had been promised. A square basin, like a main square in the middle of the town, is surrounded by cafes, bars, fine old buildings, and by the promenade of passers by. All thoughts of moving on to the ports of the Normandy Bay evaporated, and we settled in to enjoy a long stay in this ideal spot. If we enjoyed sitting and sipping our coffee or cognacs in the midst of these surroundings, it is fair to say that *Privateer* gave pleasure to a number of the promenaders coming round every evening, and figured in a number of photographs and one or two water-colours—Honfleur is a Mecca for water-colour painters. We did not mind the interest being taken in us, and attempted to answer the questions directed at us. We established friendly relations with the Harbour master, an old fisherman who walked painfully along the shore with that rolling gait of old salts, but swung himself down our shrouds with great agility every morning at rum time. I was doing quite a bit of work on *Privateer,* even at that early stage of my ownership I had abandoned the idea of seasonal fitting out and laying up, and then as later regarded the process as a continuous one. I was pleased to have this excuse for a mid-morning break, and very honoured when M. Garoche brought his grandchildren along to meet me on our last Sunday morning. When we left Honfleur after a fortnight's stay, there was no way I was allowed to pay any harbour dues.

But we were not for long the only old gaffer in port. Soon after our arrival there came in that fine old ketch the *Girl Stella*. Although she wintered in Tollesbury, she was at the 'other yard', Drake Brothers, and I had never met the owner. Frank Mulville had arrived straight from his triumph that year at the East Coast Old Gaffers race. The next year Frank made the ambitious passage to Cuba which he describes in *In Granmas Wake,* only to lose the boat in a harbour shipwreck in the Azores on the way home.

Another old gaffer that came in from the South Coast was the *Romilda*. Fred Hillier maintained her in fine order and did a lot of cruising in her; it was a few years later that he was struck down with a fatal illness, and the poor old *Romilda* left to deteriorate in a mud berth.

The warm waters that lapped round the basin were a splendid breeding ground for barnacles, and when it was time to go I realised that we were carrying a fine crop on our hull. There was a space just outside the entrance to the inner harbour where there was room for *Privateer* to lean against the wall and sit on a hard bottom, so when the time came to lock out I secured here and waited for the tide to go out. I should have looked at this spot a little more carefully; as the tide began to ebb and I started to scrub it became clear that there was a sewage outfall directly astern of us, which kept up its flow all through the day. There was nothing for it, I had to get her clean before the passage home. When I had finished I was glad that there was a public baths nearby, and I plunged into the first of three hot baths, clothes and all.

I think these more or less cleaned me up, but *Privateer*'s garboards were still smelling of Honfleur for a very long while.

On our return trip it was once again just the two of us—myself and Will. Will was a fine crew and would stay on the helm all day if necessary; but I thought I should draw the line at having him keep watches at night, so we tried to adapt ourselves by harbour hopping and avoiding where possible more than one night at sea. Our first day took us to Fécamp, but not without incident. In the steep seas off Cap d'Antifer the dinghy's painter carried away, and we had to make two attempts before we could get a warp secured and tow with a proper length. Towing a dinghy is always, of course, a problem in a sea, but I had not then realised what a difference it made to have a long tow. Although our pram was only 8 ft long, there was really no way it could be carried on board. With a wind gusting up to 6, Will and I were glad to turn into Fécamp—especially since it blew up to a full gale during the night. We stayed a day in harbour while the wind blew itself out, and took the opportunity of getting ourselves a better dinghy painter.

The next day, with a light Southwesterly wind we made a comfortable leg to Dieppe and secured in the outer harbour for the night. Lying on my bunk that night I kept being woken by drunken voices singing such ditties as 'Roll out the Barrel' *in English*. I wondered if I was imagining this, but in the morning discovered that this was the twenty-fifth anniversary of the Dieppe raid, and a large party of survivors had come over to celebrate.

To take full advantage of the flood, we made a very early start, and reached slowly along the coast in worsening visibility. A heavy drizzle reduced visibility to about a mile. We had last fixed at Le Treport and hoped to cross

the estuary of the Somme and sight Boulogne. At last out
of the murk loomed a huge hotel or block of flats, which
I had noticed on the way out at Camiers. Encouraged by
this fix we pressed on for Boulogne, but the tide was
ebbing now and we could not make it round the wall of
Boulogne harbour until after dark, and even then only
with the help of the engine. The next day we rested in
harbour, and met the Oxbys, now the owners of an
interesting schooner which they keep in Brittany. At that
time they had a boat which Dick said he was going to sell
'as soon as he was the owner'. Our last leg to Dover was
straightforward, with a rising wind we made it from
Gris Nez to Dover Harbour in three and a half hours. We
went through to the inner harbour; our first cruise was
over.

CHAPTER VII

Accessories to the Act

Immediately on our return from Honfleur I went to Thomas Foulkes and bought two items. The first was an Aldis-type lamp of somewhat doubtful origin. However, whatever its age it sent—and still sends—a fine concentrated beam of light and enables me to chat up passing ships or harbour controls. I suffer from the defect of all rusty Morse operators—I can send much faster than I can read, so conversations tend to be a bit onesided. But for years our first line of defence against unwatchful ships has been well-directed 'A's' until they take some notice.

The other gadget was a radar reflector. This was also a surplus product, and had I think been supplied to American airmen in case they ditched and found themselves in a rubber dinghy in the middle of the Pacific. It was an odd umbrella-like object, which unfolded into some spidery tendrils which swung about in the rigging. Of course I have never seen what this looked like on a radar scan, but it must have had some sensational effect, as ships that came anywhere near us used to circle around and shine searchlights on us. If it solved the original problem of our radar 'invisibility' it created another problem, as it is very distressing to be circled round at night. Finally its waving arms moulted and we invested in one of the more normal type of reflectors. I once asked to go up on the bridge on a packet boat going over to the Channel Islands from Weymouth, and their radar scan was full of yachts with similar reflectors, which made a thoroughly recognisable blip at about four miles.

For many years those were the only gadgets on *Privateer,* along with the Seafarer which I found indispensible. After several trouble free years, when the Seafarer did go wrong it was as we were coming up to Poole Harbour, where it was made. We took it ashore to Electronic Laboratories, where two friendly mechanics started giving it a going over. I watched anxiously as they replaced one part after another; then they decided to scrap the old mechanism altogether and replace it with a new one, and as they were doing this one of them noticed that the original cause of all the trouble was a hairline crack in the casing which had let the water in. So now it had a new casing as well as the whole of the electrics (I believe they kept the original rotator). I could see all my holiday money going to pay for this, but they waved it aside and wouldn't take a penny for what they described as 'routine repairs'. The only other time I had any trouble with it was when a rat got aboard in Heybridge Basin and ate the coaxial cable close down to the transducer. It was impossible to make a join here, far down in a hole in the cement under her ballast, and I had to put *Privateer* ashore and dig out the old transducer. It was worrying to see a round piece of daylight below you down there, and I quickly put in the new transducer and filled up the hole with pitch.

One gadget that I would have liked to acquire was a very traditional piece of equipment—a Patent Log. It always seems odd that this simple mechanism should cost three times as much as the complicated electronic gear of the Seafarer, so for years we used Dutchman's logs. A better method of gauging the speed was to look astern at the pram dinghy; when going really fast this used to lift up and expose its bottom, and we always promised that we would calibrate it with a series of lines, 4, 5 and 6 knots. When going a steady five knots, say, there is no great difficulty about Dead Reckoning; the trouble comes when you have been ghosting through the night with occasional wafts of wind and uncertain if your speed had averaged half a knot or twice as much. When we finally got ourselves a Walker Log, we wondered how on earth we had ever managed without one.

Long before this we had acquired a Seafix, an incredibly useful and inexpensive set. This is reassuring when crossing the channel or North Sea, but really comes into its own when there is fog about. It takes some while to get used to separating out the signals, but once you have the knack it is surprisingly accurate. But this fine gadget, and the Patent Log were both far in the future.

The gear that we inherited included a Simpson Lawrence winch on a pad on the foredeck; my only complaint with it is that it is designed to bring in the anchor chain straight down into the chain-locker, which is not what is wanted. First the chain must be flaked down on the deck to be washed, and this involves using your fingers uncomfortably close to the working part. I got them caught once, but never again. There are also two splendid winches, one either side of the cockpit, for the jib sheets. When my crew were usually young children they were almost essential; but now with adult crew we manage without them as a rule. Also, I find I now tend to change down to Number Two jib before it blows up, whereas in earlier days we only had the Number One and a diminutive storm jib.

When I bought her *Privateer* had no new fangled man-made rope, all her running rigging was natural fibre. I tried to maintain this standard of purism for a number of years, but it has become increasingly difficult and expensive to do this and now it is only the jib sheets that are a beautiful white cotton and easy on the hands.

Pike and Jarman had passed on to me a hurricane lamp for an anchor light and a Tilly for lighting the cabin. These, or their replacements are still what we use, though we have added a lamp in a gimbal over the galley which is quick to light. For a long while we had no heating, but after laying up for the first few winters we decided to keep going throughout the year, and then a heater of some sort was a must. Will found a solid fuel stove at a chandlers in Brightlingsea and we found a chimney for it on a rubbish dump. That lasted for a good while before rusting away, and it has now been replaced by a 'Potbelly', a diminutive stove which is easier to control. With the old one it was hard to restrain it and once we had a good fire going the cabin was soon far too hot and all the doors and portholes would have to be opened to stop the place becoming an oven.

A chapter on *Privateer*'s gadgetry is bound to be a short one; I ought to mention one that was a gift in our first year. It's a match box dispenser, a small wooden fitting about ten inches long and a couple of inches wide which hangs opposite the galley, indicates our angle of heel and ensures that there is always more than one box of matches ready to light the primus, the navigation lamps, the hurricane lamp or the Tilly. It has fallen apart, been glued up again, is held together now with rubber bands but still works. I've never seen one in a chandlers anywhere, but I'll keep looking.

The pram dinghy that came with *Privateer* was a lightly built clinker dinghy and towed reasonably well;

it was a bit on the small side, as in those days we often seemed to have six or seven hands on board at a time, and the dinghy only held three of adult size. A worse fault was its habit of opening out, as we kept it out of the water in Frost & Drake's yard. Its best attribute was that it looked an appropriate tender for the old gaffer, but we began to weigh other factors more heavily against this and finally sold it in Calais to an American. Instead we bought a Sportyak, whose merits were almost exactly the opposite. No-one could say that the Sportyak, which is square and made of plastic, was easy on the eye, but it had all the other advantages. It had built-in buoyancy, would carry five or six adults in smooth water, towed easily without playing some of the tricks that a normal dinghy will be up to, and unlike the pram, required no maintenance. More than once I lost it, once in the Braasemeer outside Amsterdam one dark night, where by an extraordinary piece of luck we turned back and found it; the second time in West Bay, when we picked it up without difficulty. The third time was off the Owers in a rough sea, and where it seemed lost for good. But it was brought in the next day by a friendly fisherman from Littlehampton and returned home on the top of a Mini.

Privateer has not been designed to carry a boat on her deck, which is I suppose the only really satisfactory solution to the problem of tenders. We used to put the old pram on the foredeck sometimes, but this meant it was almost impossible to work the jib sheets, and no way could the anchor be dropped until it had been removed. Any traditional dinghy that was big enough to carry a crew of four or five would be far too big to stow aboard; and would also be a cause of anxiety when towing. We had considered an inflatable, but these are not supposed to row easily, and it is I should imagine difficult to lay a kedge out to windward with one. The dilemma is of course a common one, and I think originates with the tendency for cruising yachts to carry more crew for their size. Thus, in the 1930s *Privateer* would rarely have expected to carry more than two or three aboard, and so a small tender would have been adequate. Nowadays, boats of twenty feet often have four aboard; other than an inflatable, a tender to carry four would be a bit disproportionate. So, a lot of boats sail around with tenders that are really too small, and in the rough river anchorages of the East Coast this leads to disasters.

Our solution to this has been the Sportyak, acceptable on all grounds save the aesthetic. But, with the children growing up and weekend cruising frequently being just Pat and me, I had the idea of finding a way round the problem for *Privateer*. Ever since her cabin was raised and the doghouse installed, it has been impossible to fit any normal dinghy under the boom and on top of the cabin. But, I thought to myself, what about an *ab*normal shaped one? With the aid of some hardboard I made a sort of skeleton pram that would fit under the boom. The length was limited to 6′6″, not unreasonable for a pram dinghy for two, the beam was no difficulty, in fact it had to be fairly wide to go over the skylight. It was the height which was the problem, and the shape had to be flat bottomed and with low freeboard. I determined to go ahead and make a clinker built pram which would be appropriate for an old gaffer of character.

The odd shape and flat bottom posed a lot of building problems, and some of her planks are a funny shape to say the least; I built them round moulds that more or less followed the intended shape, though some of the beam amidships got lost on the way and the sides are straighter than intended. I had a lot of trouble steaming the oak frames, as they kept on breaking while being cramped in. Later I discovered that this was not because of lack of steaming, but because there was a fault in the grain. With some new battens I did better. Another design problem arose because the dinghy could only have fixed thwarts forward and aft; the midship thwart had to come out to enable the dinghy to sit over the skylight. Construction has been a slow and painful process; when at last the dinghy was completed we took it off on the roof-rack and tried it on. It fitted! This was a great surprise to everyone, but there the dinghy sat bottom-up on the coachroof, enclosing the skylight and with about a quarter-inch of clearance below the boom. Never mind that it leaked like a basket, that could soon be put right; perhaps it needed to take up, or at worst a few kilos of pitch would fix it. I thought we had solved our tender problem for good; when sailing about the East Coast we would tow the Sportyak, which gives no trouble there anyway. When going foreign we would take the little pram and there would be no worries about the tow.

My satisfaction did not last very long. As we sailed out of Tollesbury and into the main river we met up with all the traffic in and out of West Mersea. We couldn't see a thing. The dinghy neatly occupied the entire space under the mainsail, and if we wanted to see what was ahead of us we had to climb out of the cockpit on the leeward side, duck under the boom, have a look-see, and return to the helm. The dinghy now sits in the garden, and I tell myself that it was good practice building it. Meanwhile the Sportyak continues to follow us on our voyages.

CHAPTER VIII

More Cruises

Every year after our first passage, to Honfleur, we managed to 'go foreign' for our main summer holiday. Our next voyage was to Holland, but I see from my log that we took the long way round, by Ramsgate and Dunkirk, to avoid the North Sea crossing. I have always had a very healthy respect for the North Sea which for reasons which others have explained to me has the ability to kick up a very nasty short sea which can give a yacht a bad time. On this first trip to Holland I had both boys along, and we took our time working up the Belgian coast and past the mouth of the Scheldt. When we were off the Hook we got a fine breeze for a change, and a fair one at that. We seemed to take an excessive time approaching the entrance to the Hook. After we had been stemming the ebb for about six hours and it showed no signs of abating, I consulted Reeds and discovered that the Maas was in the habit of ebbing for nine hours or more. It only dawned on me then that the Dutch had skilfully disguised the river's true identity by calling it the Maas, and that this was nothing less than the Rhine, bringing the melted snows and torrents of the Alps down through the narrow entrance at the Hook. At long last the ebb slackened, and we shot in and up to Rotterdam, where we berthed at the Royal Nederlands basin. The next day I found a bookshop with some folding charts of the Inland Waterways, and a girl assistant kindly explained to me the symbols for opening bridges, clearance heights and locks, suggesting a suitable course to get to Amsterdam. The engine was a bit delicate at this time, having a tendency to boil if left running, so that at every bridge and lock-gate, we would be lying alongside all ready to start up the engine as soon as the lights went green. Rotterdam bridge and the lock into the Leck were our first experience of this type of thing, and we bungled both badly; by the time we reached the bridge it was already beginning to shut and I thought it unwise to argue. I gradually got better with my timing, but an uncertain and slow engine could always present problems. I envied the light displacement yachts which spun round in a few seconds and charged through the opening bridges; if I misjudged the opening and arrived too early by the time I had circled right round to try again the bridge would be shut in my face. I followed the main route up to Amsterdam that goes along the edge of Skipol airport, and found that we could reach most of the way with mainsail only. As we came to a bridge I would start up the engine at the last possible moment and then drop the sail. A slight turn in the canal meant that we could not fetch and we had to rely on the motor, steam pouring out of the outlet. At least with the wind on the bow I had no problems about bringing up before the locks or bridges—a more or less insoluble problem with a stern wind. Before Amsterdam the canal opens out into a wider waterway, with an attractive river frontage of trees and islands, then right into the town itself there comes a series of half-a-dozen bridges, one after the other, with maybe a few cables between each. Here the opening of the bridges is synchronised to allow a convoy to go straight through. This is an excellent scheme, but it makes no allowance for *Privateer,* her engine going as fast as I dare allow it to run, limping astern of the rest of the convoy, with a lot of barracking from impatient cyclists and animated gestures from the controllers of the bridges. We tried to look both helpful and unconcerned, but were heartily relieved when we were through all this lot and moored in the Singel. Beyond that is the ultimate in bridges, the great swing bridge which carries the entire mainline track into Amsterdam Railway Station, and which opens only once, and that at ten minutes to two o'clock at night.

It was relaxing after that to sail down the wide expanse of the Nordsee Canal, with only one bridge interrupting our progress. We drifted gently down to Ijmuiden and out into the North Sea. By this time we were getting very close to the end of our holiday, so there was no question of going down the coast the way we had come up. All my suspicions of the North Sea were soon to be confirmed; we were no sooner out of sight of land than the calm gave way to a stiff breeze and then to a hard blow. We charged off into the night, concerned only to keep our offing in this onshore wind. I lost all track of where we were steering and concentrated on easing *Privateer* through the waves as best I could and giving any shipping as wide a berth as possible. Both boys were affected by the nasty sea that got up but struggled manfully to keep going as long as they could. The wind blew itself out during the night and the morning found us, looking a bit storm-tossed, but sailing gently South East in an attempt to get back to a friendly Dutch port as soon as we could. We spotted a large buoy, closed it and found that we were in the main channel to the Hook. This time I knew what to expect from the ebbing Maas, and we duly docked in the Tug Harbour, said goodbye to *Privateer* and caught

An early start to catch the tide.

the packet boat home.

When I came back with a friend called Norman for crew a week or two later, we found that *Privateer* had suffered more damage in the Tug Harbour than she had in the buffeting outside; someone had rammed her bowsprit and broken it in half. We came back a sloop instead of a cutter, but fortunately the wind was kind to us and we had a quartering breeze all the way and an easy passage across to Brightlingsea. The only hazard that I recall on the return trip was that when we got back to Tollesbury we had to ride my motorbike back to London. Norman is large, and the bike was not built to carry pillion passengers of his size. In later years we were often to return to Holland and worked the waterways all the way up from the Middelburg canal off the Scheldt up to Amsterdam and from there through the Ijsselmeer up to the north. But the next year's cruising was to bring a development that was to have considerable influence on *Privateer*'s story.

CHAPTER IX

Chartering

SAILING HOLIDAYS, east coast based, with skipper. Four berths, £15 p.w. each. Ring 01-387 6073 (days).

The discerning reader will have noticed that this story is like all the accounts they have ever read about owners of old boats in one respect at least; I was hard up. Buying a nine-tonner like *Privateer* had stretched my finances to the limit, and it was not through perversity that I made do with an engine that didn't work half the time, with sails that were apt to tear, and with old gear that needed replacing. I managed for many years to run *Privateer* on the proverbial shoestring, but there would come a time, I knew, when I should have to lay out some money. Where was this going to come from?

I remembered how I used to sail charter yachts, in the days before *Privateer,* and how I would pay thirty or forty pounds a week for this, out of season too. Of course, I could not trust anyone with *Privateer,* that was out of the question; not for me the arrangement Dick had made with his Eventide, handing her over to Blackwater Charters for a whole season and sailing her only when she wasn't booked. But, I thought, if I chartered her complete with skipper, I should be able to ask that much more. I began to count the chickens, and raised the idea with Frank Mulville, the sort of man to know about these

69

A slow approach to Dunkirk with charter party.

things.

Frank was horrified; he had not chartered himself, but was full of terrible stories of would-be charterers who had sailed to seek their fortunes in the West Indies and had suffered every degradation before giving up in despair. Frank advised me in the strongest possible terms not to consider chartering, and warned me solemnly that I should regret it if I didn't heed his advice.

Of course we don't ask our friends for advice in order to take it, so I went ahead and put a notice in *The Times,* offering a week or two's holiday at what seemed a competitive rate, and implying a slightly flattering picture of *Privateer.* I had ready a duplicated sheet, again containing no untruths, or hardly any, and setting out the details.

There were quite a few replies to the original advertisement, but less to the duplicated follow-up. I had paid this much attention to Frank's warning, that I resolved to be careful about whom I took. So as a result of telephone conversations I eliminated anyone that I didn't take to immediately. This left me with one or two weekenders, but for the August holiday the booking was for two girls Pat and her friend Christine, to be joined in the second week by another girl, Jill.

For some reason *Privateer* was not on her mooring then but had been left up in the Twizzle at Walton; I collected Pat and Christine at the London terminus and drove them up to Walton. *Privateer* had I suppose been left at Walton in a hurry, and without time to clear up properly. She must have been in a bit of a shambles, and I saw the disgust on the girls' faces as they emptied the teapot, full of mouldy tea-leaves, over the side. We met at Walton a young American boy (the cousin of a friend) who was coming with us, and he didn't help by first getting stuck in the Walton Carnival and keeping us all waiting for hours, and then asking if anyone had any grass with them.

In fine and almost wind-less weather we had made our way gently to Mersea, then on across the estuary, where we drifted on the ebb towards Herne Bay pier. We all had a swim alongside, and when the tide turned we anchored; there was not a breath of wind. The American lad, Mel, either because of the shortage of grass, or because he didn't take to this slow and stately way of life—for whatever reason, he asked to be put ashore. Pat rowed him to the end of the mile-long pier, he scrambled up a gangway and we never saw him again. After we had done this, I noticed that there was a bit missing in the middle of the pier and worried that we might have marooned Mel, but there was no sign of him, and in fact we heard later that he had managed to get across the gap and onto the mainland. However, this was not the end of his troubles; an alert policeman had seen him scrambling ashore and had asked him to identify himself. Mel had no passport with him and spent some time in the local police station before his English cousins could be reached on the phone and vouch for him.

We meanwhile remained becalmed at anchor for the night, but were woken early by sounds of frapping. A wind had got up, and so we wasted no time but raised the anchor and made our way swiftly through the channel between Hook Sands and the Kentish shore, past Margate and round the corner of the North Foreland. Here there was a fine beam wind, later backing slightly to make a quartering breeze of force 5 or 6. By lunchtime we were passing the South Goodwin Lightship and making direct for Calais. With a rolling sea and a wind on the quarter it is impossible to hold a course exactly, but Pat made a very good job of steering in what is the only situation where *Privateer* is heavy on the helm. By one of those happy coincidences the large pillar buoy that lies off Calais turned up dead ahead of us, and I acquired a reputation for accurate nagivation that Pat has never abandoned despite all the evidence to the contrary. Exactly three hours and ten minutes after passing the Goodwin Light we were sailing between the twin piers of Calais harbour, the fastest channel crossing I have made in *Privateer* so far.

We moved into the inner harbour, where we were joined by Jill, while the wind outside blew up and then away altogether. We made a slow passage on to Dunkirk, where we entered harbour so slowly that we could row the tender off and take a photo of *Privateer* against the stones of the breakwater. As can be seen *Privateer* was wearing her brand new Number 3 jib, a tiny stormsail which was the only one we had now, not counting the so-called Genoa, or acting-spinnaker. From Dunkirk we moved on to Nieuport, where we sailed up the narrow gut and careened on the mud. It was a messy place for scraping, but the girls waded in gamely although this activity was not I think in my brochure. We soon had the barnacles biting the dirt.

We came off the mud and lay alongside a Belgian boat, whose owner was also chartering. He was persuaded, with much show of reluctance, to get out his guitar and sing to us, and I have never heard a man with so much self confidence as a musician based on so little technique. I think he had only one chord, but he sang and played with such conviction that no-one seemed to notice. We moved on to Ostend, where I managed to get *Privateer* through the entrance to the boat harbour and alongside the pontoons without using the engine. Perhaps the girls thought this was a display of seamanship, but the real reason was that it was a safer method than with our uncertain engine. From Ostend we took the train up to Bruges, one of the most beautiful cities in Europe and one that is strangely underrated. It has the necessary history for a perfect result, having been prosperous in the late middle ages, when all the houses were built, and then gone into decline, so that they were never replaced. In its heyday it was the great port to which all the English wool was sent—difficult to imagine now that it is so far from the sea.

Our leisurely progress was beginning to run us out of time; we had to turn for home. We left Ostend, with some wondering stares from some of the all-male crews of the yachts there, drifted back past Nieuport, then ran into thick fog, keeping well inshore and hoping to miss the traffic that way. Dunkirk lights showed up through gaps in the fog, and we finally worked our way into the harbour as the fog cleared and dawn broke. Here we were met by a large number of visitors, including Will, who had been staying with a French family. After a day of junketing it was time to go home. On the return journey we broke no cross channel records; it took us seven hours to get from Dunkirk to the South Goodwin, and another seven to get round the corner to Whitstable, where we anchored off the Street.

At that time my sister lived in Whitstable, and it was her constant anxiety that one day she would awake to see her brother aground on the Street, that great spit that sticks out at right angles to Whitstable. The thought of the shame this would cause her was too awful to contemplate, and I always supposed this was why she moved inland. Of course I never did get aground on the Street, though I did once, with my sister aboard, take the ground at high water up the Swale.

Making a very early start from Whitstable, we made our way slowly across the estuary and round to Barrow, where the wind headed us. The ebb took us as far as the south side of the Whitaker sand and no further; no way could we beat round the corner against wind and tide. I took *Privateer* as close in to the sand as I dared and anchored. We sat and watched the flood tide gradually covering the sands. With the wind about 4-5 from the North-east our anchorage was becoming more and more uncomfortable. We now looked across the choppy sea rolling over the sands to the Crouch channel, only about half a mile away from us, with the channel buoys show-ing clearly, and many craft sailing up and down. It was tempting to say the least, and I worked out the depths over the sand more than once. After four hours of flood I waited no longer, we hoisted sail, up anchor and with the wind on the beam foamed across the sands. I switch-ed off the echo sounder, there wasn't a thing I could do whatever story it told. After a few exhilarating minutes we were off the edge of the sand and into the deep water of the Crouch, where we turned hard left and found our-selves in the middle of Burnham regatta, with class after class of yachts racing up behind us, alongside us and in front of us. We surfed down the steep waves, doing about eight or nine knots over the river bed. In no time we were up to Burnham and swinging to an anchor in the quiet lee of the town. That was the end of the charter cruise, as Pat and Christine had to leave immediately, and we put them ashore on the hard as soon as we had cleared Customs. It was time to draw up a balance on the success of chartering. Looked at financially it was a dead failure; all the charterers were going to come sailing again, but next time as guests, not as paying customers. This meant that however many charters I got, if things went this way it could not be profitable. Frank had been right about that. On the other hand, looked at from other points of view, it had not turned out so badly. Pat signed on as regular crew; and in due course we got married and lived happily ever after.

CHAPTER X

The Heineken Rally

In 1973 Heinekens, the Dutch brewers ran some sort of motorboat race as a publicity stunt. Evidently this had brought them some useful footage, so they decided to hold a rally and race for sailing craft the following year. An invitation was received, via the RYA, by the Old Gaffers Association: if owners of old gaffers would send in their application form they would be enrolled on this sponsored rally. Accordingly, after the 1974 East Coast Old Gaffers Race on the last Saturday in July, there was a meeting with Heinekens to give us a briefing. We were given some Heineken flags and tee-shirts, a tray of lager for each boat, and told to start together the next morning at ten o'clock. This was a reasonable condition, so that TV and other cameras could record the fleet of forty old gaffers all starting together. The wind was kind to us, a Westerly, about 3-4, so that the whole fleet stayed fairly close together. Other boats' logs recorded that we were doing a steady 5 knots through the water and benefiting from the ebb as we went through the Wallet. *Privateer* had no spinnaker then, but we had an old nylon Genoa that I had picked up in Burnham which we put out on a 14' tent-pole and this was our nearest approach to one. We set this and slowly overhauled *Kyle of Bute,* a yacht of about 28 feet, and kept more or less level with the fine Dutch barge-yacht, the *Saskia van Rijn.* We also over-

hauled a Bermuda rigged boat, the *Blue Shoal,* familiar
to all readers of Jack Coote's invaluable *East Coast
Rivers.* With the tide turning against us we reached the
North East Gunfleet buoy and turned for the Sunk light
vessel. We passed that at half past three, only five and a
half hours out from Stone.

We held our 'spinnaker' as long as we could, making
good somewhere between 5 and 6 knots now and
experiencing some quite rough seas over the Gabbard. It
was time now to get the spinnaker in, at about 5 o'clock,
and we followed the rest of the fleet in working round to
a course of about 100 degrees, to avoid a gybe. We missed
the six-o'clock weather forecast, and this explained why
we didn't reef, though several of the boats ahead pulled
round into the wind to take in a reef. There was a bunch
of some of the faster boats ahead, and another bunch
around us; with this steady stern-wind we were advancing
in formation as if we were all locked together. Astern of
us were some smaller boats, some very tiny for this rough
sea and quite heavy blow. During the night it blew
consistently Force 6 or 7 and we must have been making
remarkably good progress all the time. During the early
hours we picked up the loom of more than one of the
Dutch lights, but I could not believe my own eyes, and
thought this must be some trick of refraction. As it got
lighter, at 0500 we picked up a clear bearing on Goeree
Light tower; I still couldn't take in that we had already
reached the far side. We had seen masthead lights all
around us during the hours of darkness, and these now
materialised into a bunch of five or six craft, including as
before the easily recognisable *Saskia.* The wind was now
falling away, and as we turned up the Dutch coast towards
Ijmuiden we had a breeze of 3 or 4 behind us. The flat
coast of Holland gave us nothing to get a fix on until at

0900 we used the Seafix to get bearings on Hook and Ijmuiden. We got out the spinnaker again and kept on till noon when we could see the chimneys of Ijmuiden, as well as the haze of yellow smoke above them. As the wind fell away we were passed by several of the yachts that we had been keeping company with all the way from the Blackwater; nearly everyone has more canvas than we do.

The last part of this passage was very gentle, and we sailed through the outer harbour lights of Ijmuiden and at 1520 locked into the smallest of the three locks that lead into the Nordsee Canal, alongside *Band of Hope.* That was twenty-nine hours from Stone in the Blackwater, and a time I was sure we would never better. One of the yachts which had streamed a log gave the distance as 158 miles, making an average speed of 5½ knots. Inside the canal we continued to sail, although the wind was dropping away to light airs; most of the fleet was ahead of us now, many using their engines as they neared Amsterdam. There is a big railway bridge about halfway to Amsterdam, which normally opens every half hour or so, but as luck would have it this bridge decided to take a couple of hours rest after we missed the six o'clock opening, so we didn't arrive in to Amsterdam until after dark.

Heinekens had cleared a long wharf for us in the Ertshaven, round the corner from the main town. Usually when in Amsterdam we go into the Sixhaven, which is in effect the only yacht harbour in Amsterdam, and which is, shall I say, not entirely worthy of the capital of the Netherlands. The only alternative to the Sixhaven is the little yacht harbour on the town side of the river, just by the Central Railway Station, where the wake of every passing barge, steamer or ferry sends all the boats inside into paroxysms of rolling. This quay in Ertshaven was rather far from the town centre, but this was no worry as Heinekens had laid on an hourly bus service. I had crossed with my full crew of Pat, Chris and William; we were now joined in Amsterdam by two visitors, Arthur and Freddie. It was fine weather, and we managed not to crowd each other too badly as we lay in harbour and enjoyed the hospitality of Heinekens and our own sight-seeing. We were also being sight-seen, and with the help of Heineken's publicity machine the newspapers were full of pictures of the English Gaffers, and streams of Dutch visitors came to admire what was certainly an impressive sight. From the *Marguerite T,* a Bristol Pilot Cutter in beautiful order, to the tiny sixteen-footer that had come all the way with us, we were a decidedly interesting bunch of boats.

Not quite all had crossed over according to plan. One yacht, not an old gaffer but a bermuda boat of ply construction, had run aground on the sand outside Ijmuiden harbour on the way across. What had happened was this; the skipper had been keeping watch during the night and was coming in towards the lights of Ijmuiden; thinking it was time he got a rest he woke up his crew, turned the boat over to him and went below. Unfortunately in the course of this change of watch there was a confusion between the light on the harbour mole and a light above a golf club outside the town. The Dutch press was full of the rescue attempts, which ended with Heinekens hiring a bulldozer and lifting the boat bodily out of the sands to safety.

The other story that we heard was the saga of the rescue boat. This was Tom Polden's fishing launch from Heybridge Basin, which was carrying all the cups and other prizes across to Amsterdam. By the time she reached the Sunk she was rolling horribly, and before the Gabbard, very wisely decided to turn back. The rest of us, with sails to keep us steady, carried on regardless. Unfortunately, the rescue boat put in to Orford haven where there is no telephone, and there ensued a game of hide-and-seek in which there was talk of hiring light aircraft, and the prizes were eventually brought over only just in time to be handed out.

As part of our contract with Heinekens we ate two enormous dinners, visited their brewery and spent our last day racing in the Ijsselmeer. This had an unexpected result, and the Tollesbury boat *Greenshank,* carrying more sail than usual and I think an extra mast, won the race outright—a triumph she has not since repeated. *Privateer* did even worse than usual in this race; we had engine trouble and arrived late at the start, then I hoisted our Jenny as a jib and what little wind there was blew her head right away from it. I regret to say that we did not even complete the course, as we were most anxious to get back through the railway bridge and into harbour for the après-race celebrations.

During the huge Dutch meal that was laid on for us, my crew increased from six to seven. My daughter Cathy had decided to cut short a holiday elsewhere and came back via Amsterdam, where she had spent all day trying to find us. She succeeded just in time for this prize-giving feast.

After that the bonanza was over, and we were required to leave the Ertshaven at once. We had a headwind in the Nordsee Canal and had to beat all the way, being over-hauled by the Heybridge Basin boat the *Argo,* another converted Bermuda boat that had insinuated itself into the rally. We listened to the six o'clock weather forecast in the lock at Ijmuiden, alongside the old *Band of Hope,*

Long sheets in the Ijsselmeer.

then set off for what should have been an uneventful crossing.

So in many ways, it was, and just as well since there were seven of us aboard. We had to organise a strict watch system only allowing three or four at a time in our small cockpit with the rest 'on watch' down below. The wind died right away and we spent the night with an oil rig. In the early morning it swung round and gave us that rare delight, a quartering breeze which took us all day at a steady four knots across towards Harwich. With a smooth sea and a fair wind, with good visibility and a good forecast, the boys could see no reason for the skipper to be on deck and I was finally sent below to get some sleep soon after midnight. I had just got myself comfortable in a pipecot, listening to the gentle lapping of the water past her bow, when there came a call from aft. A red flare had gone off up to starboard. I found this impossible to credit on such a fine night, but before I could enter an argument, a whole series of red rockets followed. I told the boys to get a bearing and hurried on deck. Up on the horizon we could see the flames rising from the belly of a fishing boat. As we got closer we could see a continuous wall of flame about thirty feet high reaching up into the air. A small boat was passing between the stricken fishing boat and a large freighter standing by her, no doubt taking off the crew. We noted another yacht converging on the disaster, and got ready to offer help if it was needed. By the time we were on the scene, an hour or so from the time we had sighted the rockets, it looked as if the freighter was coping with the situation. We called her up on the Aldis to offer medical help if it was needed, but when we got no reply to our 'As' I thought our best contribution would probably be to clear out of the way, which we did. This happened about halfway across the North Sea and I suppose it was one of the large Continental trawlers that had caught fire; there was nothing in the British press about it, and so we shall never know what happened.

The rest of the passage was quiet, although visibility was reduced to a mile or so, with the aid of the Seafix we had little difficulty in entering Harwich despite our inability to see the Sunk Light vessel. We cleared customs in Harwich and went up to Wrabness where the railway line comes conveniently close to the river and where we could thin out our overcrowded crew. We punctured and threw overboard the last tin of lager. Our sponsored holiday was over.

Mr Taylor had made us a brand new mainsail and jib.

CHAPTER XI

Towards the Baltic

Who can say why the elvers swim all the way across the Atlantic, find the right river and make their way back to the very same creek where they were spawned? We humans lead more complicated lives, but we are told that there are deep unconscious drives that propel us towards following in our father's footsteps. Maybe it was an urge of this sort which led me to become the owner of a 32-foot boat and the cruise to the Baltic was inherent from the start. Let me explain.

In 1905 my father sold the *Nicolette,* a fast twenty-eight footer which he raced with the Blackwater Sailing Club and built the ten-tonner *Uldra* at Harris's yard in Rowhedge. He had read Slocum's account of his voyage in the *Spray* a few years earlier and like many others began to think about cruising. The appearance of *Riddle of the Sands* in 1903 pushed him in the same direction. *Uldra* was a fine yacht, seaworthy and fast. In 1906 father sailed her over to Holland, and the following year made the first of his voyages to the Baltic, the part of the world he liked best. He kept a fair-copy Log of all his voyages, so I was able, sixty-six years later to follow in *Uldra*'s wake.

Privateer had been very specially prepared for this trip. I had swung the engine out (an operation which turned out to be very simple) and Mr Hedgecock in

Maldon had given it a thorough going over. Mr Taylor
had made us a brand new mainsail and Number One
jib. We had a new mast (we did not know at the time
that this was going to give trouble so soon afterwards)
and I had checked over the running rigging. The year
was one in which William had done his O levels and
could reasonably miss the tail end of the summer term
and come away for a long holiday, and Pat also was able
to take six weeks off. I was determined to take two
months off, and arranged for mail to be forwarded while
I was away. I bought some charts, the Baltic *Pilot*, read
the classic *Falcon on the Baltic* and the more recent book
by John Seymour, *Willynilly to the Baltic* but most of all
studied my father's log books. Pat filled *Privateer* to the
Plimsoll line with tins of food. We carried gallons of
home brewed beer, cartons of long-life milk, a sack of
potatoes and no end of tupperware boxes, all syste-
matically stored and labelled. I had no idea there was so
much storage space on the boat, and realised we had
consistently under-used the spaces under the decks, under
the bunks and up forward under the pipecots. It was as
well that we took so much food with us, as some horrible
thing happened to Sterling while we were away and the
pound was a bad joke in all the countries we were going
to visit. Before we started I bought francs, guilders,
marks, krone—as many as I could afford to last us the
journey.

  We made a leisurely start on this cruise, partly because
the winds were light, also perhaps because we felt we had
so much time ahead of us we need not hurry. Pat could
not join us for a week, and besides Will I had my daughter
Cathy to help us on our way. Our first day out from
Brightlingsea, despite a very early start we had only got
to the West Barrow, at the end of the Maplin channel, by

10 o'clock. From there we drifted slowly across the Estuary, past the Shivering Sand Ford (noon) and then to pick up the West Last Buoy on the Kentish side at four o'clock. By eight in the evening we were off Ramsgate, and it was again dead low water. After such a long day we fancied getting into harbour and I worked out the depths carefully. As it was a flat calm evening it seemed worth a try, so we motored gently towards the harbour entrance and went aground between the piers. when *Privateer* touches like this it is of course her heel that is on, that end of her drawing about 4'6" and the forward end of her keel about 2'9". If a weight of about twelve stone is perched on the end of her bowsprit, thirteen feet forward of her stem, the resultant leverage lifts her heel about two or three inches. I scrambled out along the bowsprit and looked round to see if she was moving at all. What I did see was the sea below me covered with highly coloured sheets of paper of different sizes. My back pocket had emptied our entire stock of foreign currency onto the surface of the sea. Will brought the dinghy up quick and we collected every last note; we spread them out to dry in the cabin, and later inside the log or in between the pages of my passport. Notes kept surfacing every time we crossed a frontier.

The tide was on the turn and we were only on for a quarter of an hour; but during this time two local boats came up and offered to tow us off with dire warnings of the danger we were in. We thanked them, laid a kedge and pulled off and into the outer harbour. I made a note to keep to the landward side of the middle of the entrance next time. Since then there has been much dredging here and I think this advice is now superfluous.

After a night in Ramsgate harbour, always an expensive and uncomfortable place to be, *Privateer* set off for

Dover the following morning. The log records that it took all of ten and a half hours to get down to Dover. It would take years to get to the Baltic at this pace, especially as we were not even making progress in the right direction. Up early the next day to cross the channel; with the help of some light airs we took twelve hours to get to Gris Nez, by which time the tide was running westabout. There was no way we could beat the tide to Calais, so we drifted slowly down to berth in Boulogne just as it was getting dark.

Discouraged by these long-winded drifts in the wrong direction, we spent a day in Boulogne harbour, then managed to get to Calais the day following. Here we said goodbye to Cathy and put her on the packet boat, and welcomed Pat who arrived later in the day. The cruise had begun in earnest, or so we hoped.

In fact we had to make three attempts to get out of Calais. The tides were such that we left about nine o'clock in the morning; the first day we ran into a stiff north-easter. Wind was against tide and a nasty sea was soon getting up. We ran back to Calais and picked up the same buoy in the outer harbour. The second attempt the next day found the wind still north-east, but now it was force One or so. We tried to make some headway but when the tide turned we were still in sight of Calais tower, so turned back and ran gently for Calais harbour with nothing to show for the day except a couple of unwary mackerel. Only at the third attempt did we get a fair wind and make it all the way to Dunkirk. After a night at the pontoon there our luck changed and we made a fine hop of 52 miles to berth at Breskens the next morning. From there we decided to take the more interesting inshore passage, and locked in at Flushing the next day to motor up to Middelburg. There was a clock calm and we were all, including the engine, feeling the heat a bit. Will and I took a line ashore and tried some trekking. This was the method used by *Uldra* for this canal in 1907, she having no engine. It was no strain to maintain a steady 2½ knots, though the tow line had to be lifted over the surprised heads of anglers sitting along the bank. This method of making headway had evidently gone out of fashion. We were so conscious of being behind schedule that we had no time to look at the charming little port and town of Veere, but started the motor and ran our way up to Veersemer, now an inland sea.

This is a favourite place for pleasure boating, a stretch of Broad with a well buoyed channel winding through shallows on either side. It is a sanctuary for birds, and they build their nests undisturbed on the rushy islets which abound. We found a place to anchor off the fairway and spent a peaceful night—only one other boat with two honey-mooners was in sight. The inland sailors of Holland are sparing in their use of the anchor, and as the evening came on had all withdrawn to their pontoon berths.

The next morning we again had an easterly wind, very light, and beat slowly up the channel, too early for the busy traffic that fills it up later. By breakfast time we had locked into the big Zandcreek Lock which takes you out to the tidal Ostscheldt. From here we beat gently through the Keeten channel, then a fetch up the Maastgat and into a 'Vluchthaven' at Zijpe. This spacious refuge we thought was not much in use, but later in the evening more yachts arrived and a barge or two.

With light airs, and those from the wrong direction, we were making slow, if steady progress—fourteen miles for each of the last two days. Again we had light easterly airs, but left the harbour at Zijpe to catch the flood which took us up to the Krammer channel. Here at last we got some wind, squalls of it from dead ahead as we slowly made our way up the winding channel, avoiding the barges by borrowing beyond the buoys either side. The squalls soon died down, and we started the engine to take us into the lock that led into the Hollandisch Diep. Through this and a couple of hours motoring before we came to the turn up to Doordrecht—well signposted. Here at last we struck lucky with the wind, and for the first time had a strong breeze from astern to take us up to Doordrecht. This was just as well as there was a tide running quite hard against us. In this part of the world it is not always easy to tell when you are going to be in non-tidal or tidal water. Even up-to-date charts have a provisional look about them, like road maps with future motorways already marked in. At Doordrecht we arrived late and very wet. We were the wrong side of the road bridge and among the commercial traffic. As we looked for somewhere to berth, a Scottish coaster came to our aid. The master sent his only crewman down to take our lines, and soon we were enjoying a shower on the *Inganess Castle* and the hospitality of Captain Henderson and his wife. Although there are a lot of beautiful old gaffers in Holland, they are not to be found in this part of the world, being mainly in the Ijsselmeer further north. So a boat like *Privateer* attracts quite a bit of favourable attention here in the middle of Holland. The engine was indispensable for getting in and out of locks and through bridges, but we found that nearly all the time we were under sail, and the waterways were wide enough to keep well clear of the commercial barge traffic. This was less true inside the locks, and we got a nasty knock at Gouda when a barge skipper suddenly ran his prop and sent a small tidal wave across the lock to crash our bow into the side. It was quite a blow, but there was no structural damage, just another scar. The stern wind that had helped us the previous day kept us going, through Gouda and on to the Braasemeer, familiar to us from a previous voyage, and so right up to the notorious motorway bridge. Looking for a safe anchorage for the night we ran hard aground and had to take a line across to the far bank to heave off. There was enough barge traffic up and down the canal to make this difficult and hazardous. Unlike the railway bridge in Amsterdam itself, this motorway bridge does open occasionally, and we only had to wait until lunchtime to get through; from there onwards is a straightforward run, through the suburbs of Amsterdam up to the big sluis, then on in convoy under the road bridges opening one after the other to let us through into the heart of Amsterdam. Once more the long wait for the railway bridge, which opened two hours after schedule at 0345. We whiled away the time with some newly found Dutch friends and a Belgian yacht we had known before. One of our new friends showed us the way, following his masthead light, into the Sixhaven where we secured alongside a Swedish motoryacht and slept.

Later the same day, we had made a quick foray into the town but found city life too tiring and decided to take advantage of the fresh South westerly wind to press on. Less than an hour later we were at the big Dingedam bridge, and through into the Ijsselmeer. Another two hours and we were at the entrance to the Gouwzee channel, making good around six knots under mainsail and foresail, bowsprit still tucked away inboard. A difficult half-hour beating up the narrow channel to Vollendam in the dusk and then we were inside and secured to a pair of posts.

Vollendam was one of the places that father had visited in *Uldra* and he often spoke of the little fishing port on what was then the Zuyderzee, where the artists had paid for their drinks with paintings which hung in the taverns. A short visit ashore told us all we needed to know; the place was given over to tourism, with plastic buckets on sale at every shop along the seafront. There were a few fishing boats of traditional build, probably converted to power many years previously, but still carrying masts which might take a steadying sail if needed. A poster announced a race for Platbodinjachts in nearby Monickendam in a couple of days time, but we did not fancy staying in Vollendam and decided to move on straight away. The bowsprit had to be run out and rigged—quite an operation, this—and soon after midday we were on our way, to cross the Ijsselmeer. There was a fine breeze from the NNW kicking up a sea in the shallow waters of the Ijsselmeer. On our way out we were rewarded by seeing the old Dutch plaatboats sailing in ready for the forthcoming regatta. With the wind on the beam we were making splendid progress and expecting to make a fast passage across and up to Harlingen, but the pin of the gammon iron sheared, the sudden strain carried away the Wykeham Martin reel, and we had to down sail and get the bowsprit back inboard again. It now looked impossible to fetch up to the lock at Harlingen and we pointed for Stavoren, getting into the outer harbour just after dusk. During the night the wind blew up from the South west and we were woken by violent rolling. The forecast was for Force 7. We needed to get into the inner harbour at once, and all the other yachts in the outer harbour had the same thought in mind. Following one of these we ran aground, and of course immediately blew harder on. We ran a line astern to the staithe where we had been lying and with the help of two Dutchmen managed to pull *Privateer* off stern first. Somehow we got into the inner harbour without any more mishaps, leaving a steel yacht in the outer harbour tangling with a row of marker buoys. The two Dutchmen came aboard for breakfast and told us that we did not need to go up to Harlingen as we thought, but could follow the canal through from Stavoren and join up with the Frisian canal system further east. This was very good news, and we could now make use of this westerly wind to blow us through the Frisian canals at a great rate. We soon got used to the ways of the bridge keepers, who nonchalantly wait for you to sail right up close before they start to open the bridge. Once we had got the hang of this we found progress much faster, with no bringing up into the wind, taking in sail and starting motors, but just sailing through.

Our only hold-up was to run into the Frisian Sunday. In this Protestant province it is a sin to open a bridge on a Sunday. This route is not all canal, through the Sneekermer it widens into a Broad with much holiday traffic. In my father's day you could go straight through Groningen and on to Delfzyl, but nowadays you have a fixed bridge before Groningen and have to turn off a small side-canal and wind your way round into the town. The turning off was so small that we missed it, came to the motorway and had to motor back a mile or so. An old Dutch lady opened the swing bridge for us by leaning against it and let us into a ditch full of waterlilies and weed and with branches of willows brushing our cross-trees. With a fair wind still astern of us we managed to sail most of this bypass, but in the afternoon it died away and we accepted a tow from a German trading

ketch which took us fast into Groningen, and after an evening's exchange of hospitality, on to Delfzyl the next morning. Here we were glad to be sniffing the open sea again after more than two hundred miles of Dutch waterways. William calculated that we had now come 438 miles from Tollesbury; but having taken three weeks to do this did not give us a very impressive mileage. We took a day off at Delfzyl to get a repair done on the Wykeham Martin and buy some charts. Although I had bought charts for both the inside and the outside passage

past the German Frisian islands, I was of course irresistib-
ly drawn to the inside passage and we decided to follow
this part of the journey in *Dulcibella*'s wake and through
the Bants Balje channel. We locked out of Delfzyl and
sailed down the buoyed channel till we got to OT buoy
where we anchored in eight feet of water and waited for
the tide. We lay here for a couple of hours, then reached
up to the north and felt our way with the depthsounder
across the Schuiten sands, to pass the buoy at the
beginning of the Bants Balje channel at five o'clock. I am
not sure where the name originates, but it sounds neither
German nor Dutch; it evokes for me the special feeling of
the Waddensee, unlike any other piece of water I have
sailed on, with its low-lying invisible shores, long and
extremely narrow twisting channels, marked every few
yards by withies. The channels are so narrow that the
pilot books even argue about whether you should keep
the withies five yards or ten on your beam. It was as well
we had a fair wind from the Northwest, as beating along
the Bants Balje would have been impossible. We were
now slightly behind schedule for the tide, and as we had
encountered no depths less than seven feet coming over
the Schuiten, we could have cut it a bit finer and started
earlier. There was no other traffic ahead of us, but as we
reached the entrance to the Bants Balje we were passed
by a German Customs launch. We shot past the four
buoys with wind and tide behind us, then reached the
withies and followed the banisters as the channel turned
and twisted towards Norddeich. We crossed the water-
shed just fifteen minutes after High Water, and began to
pick up the ebb off Norddeich. Here the channel turns
up sharply to the Northwest, in our case straight into
the wind. We kept our eyes on the Seafarer and made
very short boards down this part of the channel, which is

slightly wider than the waterway over the sands, and is marked by buoys. We could now see the island of Nordeney ahead as the light began to fail, and we lit our navigation lamps, which promptly blew out. The only navigational hazard here was the Nordeney ferry, which came past with much whistling and on an unsteady course. The captain and crew seemed to be very happy, and the wake of the ferry was marked by empty bottles. The wind was starting to die on us, but there was still enough to take us the last bit against the ebb and into Nordeney harbour, where we secured just after dark.

It was years since I had read *Riddle of the Sands,* but so well does Childers evoke the feeling of the place that I really felt I knew the area. In fact I had misremembered my *Riddle,* and found that *Dulcibella* had used the other channel, but no matter. Except that there were no trading schooners and botters anchored off the harbour waiting for the tide, Nordeney had not changed so much since those days. The island is dominated by a very Imperial Spa which is totally in the past and has no relation to the crowds of young people, all in their uniform of PVC anoraks who could not be imagined in the vicinity of a Casino. The harbour master was very considerate and friendly, and much admiring of *Privateer;* old gaffers were none too numerous up here, in fact apart from the Ijsselmeer gaffers were rarely to be seen on any part of our voyage.

It came on to blow again, this time from the north, and we walked across the island to the north shore to see the white water over the Dove Tief channel and the rollers coming in on the beach. There were notices up everywhere about walking parties over the sands, which is the main attraction for tourists on Nordeney, but the thought of this depressed us and we decided to see the island another way by hiring a fourwheeled bicycle. We pedalled this at speed along the one road that leads between the dunes along to the eastern end of the island; there was nowhere else to go. At last the wind showed signs of blowing itself out and we were eager to get on our way. When he saw us casting off the harbour master came running down from his office to warn us not to go— I felt embarrassed by his consideration and at ignoring his advice, but the wind had dropped away to a gentle breeze leaving only a heavy swell. To get out of Nordeney we had to go round the western end of the island just before High Water, and then through the gap between the islands and up the narrow and none too straight Dove Tief channel. Here the seas were rolling in steeply and breaking on the sands on either side. As you looked out ahead you could see an uninterrupted line of breakers, but close ahead was always a clear gap where the deeper water lay. The wind was heading us through here and we used the engine to help make the very short boards and get her head through the seas. The carburettor chose this moment to get clogged up and the engine was giving signs of failing; but it took us through the worst, and the ebb tide was beginning to sluice out. At long last we were far enough away from the sands to fetch off to the North East and leave the Dove Tief astern. This was a great relief, but there was still a nasty swell left over from three days of North-westers, and with not much wind to steady her *Privateer* was rolling uncomfortably. We kept parallel to the coast one side and the shipping lanes the other, but navigation here would have been helped by more detailed tidal information. The flood tide first slowed us down, and then as we got past the Frisian islands later in the day, set us into the mouth of the Weser.

Before we started on this voyage I had been warned
about the approach to the Elbe; a British yacht had
recently been lost there, run down in the dark and sunk
without trace. Frank Mulville also warned us it was a
place to keep away from in the hours of darkness. So I
had embarked on the voyage with no other commitment
but to avoid the entrance to the Elbe at night. Naturally
we were reaching across the mouth of the Jade at 0130
aiming for the Elbe No 1. Light Vessel. At least the wind
had come up to give us a good northerly breeze, with
long sheets once we had reached the Elbe Lightship. This
was as well as the ebb had now got under way and was
trying to send us back where we had come from at a good
3-4 knots. This was one of those places where there was a
small hole in our chart system, the North Sea chart had
taken us to the Elbe Lightship, and the detailed approach
to the Elbe started about eight miles further East. This
was no great worry as the channel is lit like a motorway
with buoys either side, and we kept on the extreme
southerly edge of the channel, out of the way of the
traffic. If we thought this would keep us out of trouble
we thought wrong. A small craft, which soon turned out
to be a Police Launch, manoeuvred round to our starboard side and shone a searchlight straight at us. This
made it impossible to read the compass and difficult to
see the sea marks and lights from other vessels all around
us. We waited for a loud hailer to give us some Teutonic
instruction, telling us it was forbidden to be in that area
or whatever, but they just shone the powerful searchlight on us and said nothing. I got out the Aldis and
called them on that, but they paid no attention. The
wind and seas were now from astern and this light did
not make it any easier to keep on course and avoid a
gybe. The staring eye held us for what seemed an in-

terminable time, but at last the Police launch speeded ahead. After it had gone I relaxed a bit and went up forward; our starboard light had blown out, most likely because of the sudden jerk imparted by a rolling sea. I relit the lamp, picked up the buoys on the new chart and soon the tide was on the turn and helping us up towards Brunsbuttel and the entrance to the Kiel Canal. We locked in through the big gates at noon exactly, having made a reasonable passage of 90 miles since the previous morning at Nordeney. Just behind us in the lock was the *Moby Dick,* a Swedish motor yacht that we had got to know in the Sixhaven, Amsterdam, now on her way home. We entertained the *Moby Dick* family, who were definite fans of *Privateer,* and accepted a tow from them the next morning.

This was a very acceptable offer indeed; I had not looked forward to the prospect of motoring for 58 miles through the Kiel Canal. At our speeds it would have been impossible to do it in one day and we should have to find a half-way house for the night—even supposing our engine would stand for it. *Moby Dick* was a MFV type, perhaps 15 tons, and maintained a steady 6 knots through the canal. There was no problem in being towed at that speed, and I left it to Pat and William to take turns on the helm while I sat about and enjoyed the scenery. No-one had told me the canal ran through very pretty countryside, with willows growing on the tow path, and only one or two built up sites. There was a mass of traffic going both ways, including quite a few yachts. I noticed that in spite of the Verboten signs, many of the yachts were under sail, though no doubt running engines as well. We had paid our dues while in the lock at Brunsbuttel, and the charge of 15 marks— for a boat of 32 feet—was the same as my father paid in

A friendly tow through the Kiel Canal.

1907. (Incidentally, the agreed price for a tow was exactly the same in both years—40 marks). Towing is often a fraught business, with inexperienced tugs from people who do not allow for how much a ten tonner carries her way; but being towed by Hubert in the *Moby Dick* was a real pleasure and I ignored the fact that it was a sort of vicarious motor-boating.

We got into Holtenau just after dusk, passed through the lock and secured to the pontoons by ten o'clock, not too late for a return visit for supper aboard *Moby Dick*.

Some running repairs in Brunsbuttel.

At last we were in the Baltic—exactly one month after setting out. As we stocked up with duty frees alongside the quay at Holtenau I wondered if it would come up to expectations.

CHAPTER XII

In the Baltic

For our first day in the Baltic the weather was perfect; warm and sunny, and though we started the day early with no wind at all, there was soon a little breeze taking us up along the Jutland shore. We sailed gently out of Kiel fjord, past the Levenberg light, and round the corner to the mouth of the Schlei. Just inside the narrow entrance to the fjord lies the harbour, a friendly place with as many fishing boats as yachts in it. We had to remind ourselves that we were still—just—inside German waters, this was the last harbour before the Danish border. We lay alongside a fishing boat no longer than *Privateer* with a vast one-cylinder diesel weighing four and-a-half tons. The fishermen were Danes from Sonder-berg, and were going out that night to haul up their lines. They invited William to go with them, and there was no problem with alarm clocks. When their diesel fired it was like a big gun going off, and we packed Will off before going back to sleep. They used various methods of fishing, and according to the season fished both sides of Denmark; this time they had a long line down, and found the buoy to within ten yards' accuracy with their radar equipment.

The next day was another sunny one, with very light airs, hardly enough to get us through the narrow and rocky entrance to the Schlei. We laid a course across to

Hitching a lift in Kiel Fjord.

Skoldness and drifted that way until at midday a sudden squall came down on us and for a few minutes we were doing 6 knots. This brought us nearly to Skoldness, and we hoisted the Danish courtesy flag for the first time. The afternoon saw us beating slowly round the corner against the lightest of Easterly airs. We passed between Avenako and Lyo, then down the north side of Avenako and towards Svendborg fjord. At 1800 the wind died away completely and we dropped anchor off a small jetty, our first Danish landfall. We ate heartily aboard and then rowed ashore to explore. It was pleasant to be able to anchor, not to have to manoeuvre around crowded harbours and depend on the engine. Pleasant also to be free of harbour dues, which with the state of the Pound had been causing us financial embarrassment. The next day it was on down the narrow, well-marked channel to Svendborg. We ghosted along gently, swimming on a line astern and enjoying the sunshine; by lunchtime we were turning into the harbour, and leaving the Marina to one side, berthed in the commercial harbour. Svendborg figured largely in my father's voyaging in the Baltic. This was the place he came back to frequently and in fact left *Uldra* laid up the boat yard there for the winter. We made enquiries ashore if anyone remembered Webers boatyard and at last found a chandlery where someone recalled the name; about twenty years previously it had amalgamated with another shipyard. Sixty-six years is too long a span for retracing another's voyage, there was no chance we would meet anyone who remembered the *Uldra*.

Svendborg at least was recognisably the same town, a friendly commercial harbour; no surprise to find a training schooner lying in the roads outside. The town was extra quiet at the weekend, and we found the Customs

House shut. In fact we never managed to clear Customs for the whole of our stay in Denmark until the last port of call. We flew our yellow flag under the courtesy flag all the way.

Svendborg; no surprise to find a training schooner in the roads.

From Svendborg we intended to cross the Great Belt and follow the Smaalands, south of Zealand. We wound our way out of the harbour and through the narrow gap at the entrance to the fjord, then laid course to pass between Fyn and Langeland—the Smorstakken gap. This time we had a bit more help from the wind—a series of

rain squalls coming up from astern and driving us forward
at 5 knots or so each time. Round the top of Langeland,
then aiming between the two islands Agersø and Omø.
All this part of Denmark is fairly flat, and the title of
'fjord' conjures up quite false pictures of Norwegian
coasts. As with other low-lying islands, it's not easy to
see where the gaps are until you are quite close, and the
most visible feature of Omø was a hugh refinery which
turned out to be on Zealand the other side of the island.
With the help of the excellent buoys we followed the
channel through between the little islands, then round
the reefs and back into the harbour of Agersø on the
eastward side. A comfortable eight-hour day had brought
us on another 36 miles.

Agersø proved to be a friendly harbour, slightly overcrowded with a number of German yachts on top of the
local fishing boats. The squalls of the previous day settled
into a steady near gale from the westward, and we lay
snug in harbour for a couple of days while it blew itself
out. We used the time in making a few repairs and in
walking across the island, with its farmland not too unlike my native Suffolk. Ashore the wind was howling
through the trees and making it very clear that we were
staying put. As soon as the wind did moderate, we were
off for an early start along the Smaalands, a series of
rather narrow channels in a wide expanse of sea, but all
well marked. We noticed here for the first time some
Danish fishing boats using a substantial mainsail, bigger
than the conventional steadying sail found everywhere.

The gap we were making for is spanned by the huge
bridge at Vordingborg, which we could see for miles
ahead. We passed under it soon after 1100, and with the
day so young decided to push on. There is a choice here
between the northerly route between the 'mainland' and

Privateer's track around the Baltic.

the island of Møn, and the southerly route which passes south of Møn. Although the northerly route led directly where we wanted to go, and was the one being taken by a number of yachts, we studied our chart and took the long way round. If I had spent longer choosing charts, I might have come up with a better selection and noted that this narrow passageway needed a detailed chart if it was to be attempted. As it was I had bought the charts in a rush while going through the lock at Holtenau.

The route we chose was being used by coasters, and was itself very narrow in places. Though well buoyed, we found the wind heading us when we got down to the southern tip at Harbølle and were turning up to the north. Making short boards against a Force 2 wind was slow work, and our main concern was to keep out of the way of the shipping. We were glad to be clear of this gutway at 1500 and turn up for Klintholm, the harbour on the tip of Møn, with the wind improving as we got clear of the land. Soon we were plunging along with a stern wind, and with the Jenny set. We now developed a fixed determination to get to Klintholm before the shops shut; I think our unexpectedly early start that morning had caught us short of bread. Klintholm has two moles either side of the harbour entrance and the waves were breaking on these as we plunged towards it. A knot of people had gathered to watch our rather spectacular entrance. We had taken in the Jenny at the last moment, and I was intending to sail right into the inner harbour and come up into the wind there. As we passed between the moles, from whatever misunderstanding, the peak halyard slipped and the main was scandalised. I hoped it looked as if we had done this on purpose, and we carried on into the inner harbour before luffing up according to plan. We brought up alongside at ten to six, too late for

the shops but Pat made a successful approach to a friendly cafe and we got our bread just the same. We had made
a run of 60 miles in twelve hours sailing, some of which
was spent beating slowly through the Sound. *Privateer*
was particularly well received here in Klintholm, and
some of the knot of sightseers who had watched us come
in came along and identified themselves. These were Herr
and Frau Hammer who had lived for years in Australia
and spoke the language. They owned an old gaffer, but
there were so many regulations in force in Germany that
they despaired of commissioning her. Their story may
account for the very different type of yacht-owner we
found in the Baltic. Nearly all the yachts were German,
they were nearly all very affluent craft, the owners
strode out with yachting caps and reefer jackets, while
the crew were often uniformed; the formality was unlike
anything I had experienced elsewhere. I imagine they
were all business executives used to giving orders. It was
a long way from the casual manner of the English—or
Danes for that matter. There were very few old boats
around and if there were, it was impossible to comply
with all the regulations. Possibly the aristocratic yacht
owners of 19th century Britain would have felt more at
home with these, and vice versa.

I think these remarks about German yachtsmen are
prompted because in Klintholm they imperiously ordered
us off, and an apologetic harbour master came round to
ask us to move more than once. We got some sympathetic
looks from the Danish fishermen, but there were language
barriers here, and I did not think it tactful to speak to
them in German.

The Hammers were very kind to us, and as once more
we were stormbound for a couple of days, we were glad
to be ferried on an expedition in their Volkswagen. They

took us to the top of the chalk cliffs at Moenklint up on
the 'mainland'; this is the only high ground in the whole
of Denmark, and is most impressive, not least by contrast
with the generally flat contours. From the top we could
see East Germany, surprisingly close across the Baltic.
I hope the Hammers can one day fit out their boat and
proceed to sea.

Once more it was an early start as soon as the gale
had blown itself out. We left harbour at five o'clock, but
as usual there was no wind until mid-morning. We were
making for the Swedish port of Malmö, and with a fine
wind abeam we were up to Falsterbo by lunchtime and
hoisted the Swedish flag. We followed the huge beacons
up the Swedish coast and by six o'clock had entered the
yacht harbour of Limhamn, the marina that lies close to
the commercial harbour of Malmö. The Limhamn marina
was set up and built by three yacht clubs, and is a most
impressive man-made harbour. The ethos is that of yacht
club hospitality rather than commercial values, and we
found this an exceptionally friendly place to be. Our
first three days as visitors were for free, and we made use
of the facilities ashore. We had intended to stay a day or
two as I had a visit to make to Lund, the ancient univer-
sity town a train journey inland from Malmö.

In the Limhamn there occurred one of those incidents
in which truth is better than slapstick. I should explain
that Malmö is opposite to Denmark and not very far
away, and that the arcane liquor laws of Sweden cause an
exodus of thirsty Swedes to take the ferry over to
Denmark at the weekends. Or, if they have a boat, then
they can go over that way. It was a Sunday morning, and
two Swedes were bringing their boat up to our pontoon.
All too clearly they had come from the Danish side. They
had an 18 foot motor-sailer, and one was on the helm

while his crew lay on the foredeck with boathook out-
stretched, concentration written all over his face. There
was much shouting from aft, then he reached out as far
as he could and got the boathook round a loop ashore.
The skipper could not see too clearly what was happening
up the front end of the boat and chose this moment to
put the engine hard astern. His crew formed a human
bridge for a moment, clutched at a shroud: down came
the mast, and followed him into the water. I shall never
forget the look of puzzlement on the face of the skipper
as he looked up from his gear lever and could not see his
crew or his mast anywhere.

Our visit to Lund was a great success and we brought
back with us a young couple who were going to take
passage with us to Copenhagen. Although it is only 14
miles across, this was not one of our faster passages and
it took us all of eight hours. Even then, we had made
only Kastrup, to the south of Copenhagen.

One thing about the tides around the Essex Coast, if
they are running foul you only have to be patient for six
hours and maybe drop the hook meanwhile and you will
have a fair tide. Not so in the Strait; a faint air of wind
was blowing from the North and the current was setting
the same way. We drifted slowly south into the lee of
Saltholm island, where we could make no more progress.
Here we anchored and had a swim. In the late afternoon
we made another attempt to get across to Zealand, but
finally had to use the engine to make Kastrup. This is a
small commercial port round the back of Copenhagen,
and we spent a quiet night there watching and being
watched by the people ashore. The following day was
much the same, sunny and the lightest of airs, but the
southerly set of the current had lessened during the
night and we were able to creep up the shore inside the

Trekroner fort and towards the entrance of the main harbour. Here we met a Tollesbury boat coming out and exchanged greetings. This was the first British yacht we had seen in the Baltic. We had enough steerage way to sail into the little harbour of Langelinie. This is one of the nicest yacht harbours it is possible to imagine. It is close to the 'Little Mermaid', that is near to the centre of Copenhagen, and was clean enough to swim in. A fine old gaffer, Cornish I think, sailed out as soon as we came in— changing the guard as it were. A party of Finns wearing black eye patches welcomed us by leaping aboard. Our mileage for the day was exactly six; Will totted up to find we had come 842 in all.

None of us had been to Copenhagen before and we made the most of it; not the sleazy night life, which is very un-Danish and we were told was laid on for foreign tourists, but looking at a very elegant city, full of historical interest. I put in a couple of days visiting the bookshops, and I suppose it was an unusual way for a British publisher to make the journey; in any event we were delighted to entertain the booksellers in the Langelinie. The Danes are proud of their seagoing traditions, and have a number of fine sail-training ships—one of which lay outside Copenhagen harbour while we were there. But they seem very short of old boats like ours, and were very taken with *Privateer*.

In the little harbour we made friends with a crew of Czechs, electrical apprentices who had built their own boat, got it carried by rail to Lübeck, and cut through unimaginable barriers of red tape to undertake a cruise of the Baltic. They entertained us aboard their tiny craft with potato dumplings and other national dishes, and we had them aboard in the rather ampler accommodation on *Privateer*. We also made friends with a German yacht, which we could immediately spot as being unusual. There was an easy camaraderie between the skipper and crew, they were all young and friendly. It turned out that they were German naval ratings being taught to sail with a student earning his summer holiday keep as skipper. We got on fine once I had satisfactorily explained to them why my parallel rule had a swastika on it. (This was my one and only bit of war-loot, which had come from a yacht used to train German naval cadets before the war.)

After three days of ease in Copenhagen, it was time to move on; and we followed mankind's universal practice of avoiding a return by the same route we had come out by. We sailed north to round Zealand, and south through the Great Belt. We drifted out of Copenhagen in company with the German yacht, and after a mock battle (I fear we had inflamed them with duty free rum) they took us in tow for Elsinore. This is a charming place, despite the fact that it bears no resemblance to the towering cliffs in the Olivier film of Hamlet. The cliffs measure about sixteen feet I should estimate.

From Elsinore we sailed along the north of Zealand, and with the help of a very early start managed to get to Odden on the extreme northwest tip of the island. This was an uneventful sail, with light breezes most of the time and we thought we had done well to log 52 miles that day. There was another small gap in my collection of charts in the middle of this hop, but we did not fall into any black holes or enter any firing ranges. It was a relief to see the first land mark on the new chart.

Odden was, as the *Pilot* promised, a busy fishing port; we also found an ingenious blacksmith there and at long last got a proper pin for the gammon iron for the bowsprit. We had delayed our start due to high winds, but these lessened during the day, and we made a late afternoon start to pass through the Snekkelob and make for home. The passage is a very narrow one through the reefs that stretch off the corner of Zealand, and the Westerly wind made this no easier. But it was well marked by spar buoys, and we passed through the tiny gap and then lengthened the sheets and turned down the wide waters of the Great Belt. We made good progress during the night and by morning were not far from Omø and Agersø and crossing our outward track. After this, the wind let us down once more and first headed us, so that we were making slow boards across between Langeland and Lolland, and then died away completely. We anchored off the town of Spodsbjerg and waited for a wind. This came early the next morning, and we ghosted down the shore of Langeland, saying goodbye to Denmark in mid-morning, and laying course for the Kiel fjord, which we came to in the afternoon. At 1710 we made fast to our old berth in Holtenau.

This time we were entering the Kiel canal with no friendly Swedes to give us a tow. The wind was fresh, and dead against us. The engine did its best, but was protesting slightly at the notion of running 58 miles in these conditions. I stood on the forecastle and waved an end of a hawser. The second barge to come past slowed down, the skipper came down out of his wheelhouse, there was a minimal exchange of shouts to make a contract, he took my line, made it fast and climbed back into his wheelhouse. She seemed a large craft to work all on your own, but every now and then he would disappear down below, put on a kettle or whatever, and reappear just as we were beginning to worry about his barge slewing off course. Although I had mentioned maximum speeds, this skipper was not going to waste valuable time, and kept up a steady 7 knots. As we were right in the slip stream of his propeller, this did not make for relaxed steering; more like balancing on a tight-rope. Half way down the canal we were waved off by the police launch and came to alongside one of the sets of posts on the side of the canal. Traffic was being cleared for the passage of a giant passenger liner, being towed slowly and carefully eastwards. This at least gave us a chance to chat with our barge-skipper. He was determined to save as much money as he could before he was forced to retire, and this meant working long hours, all the days of the week and working the boat on his own to save the expense of a mate. He resented the time it took to load or unload, though this in fact was the only chance he had of sleeping. When we got to Brunsbuttel, at eight o'clock in the evening, he politely declined our offer of a meal aboard; he was going to push on to Hamburg as soon as we were through the lock.

We were going to enjoy a night's rest before starting for home, and set off the next morning with the usual fitful breeze. We drifted down on the ebb and eventually reached Cuxhaven. Here we followed the sailing directions and luffed into the Aussenhafen, which was clearly deserted; we tried further down where there was a yacht 'club' and a small harbour on the site of a sewer outlet. No doubt great things were going to be done to this place, but there was little in the way of facilities except a till on the office desk. We went ashore to look at Cuxhaven, a town which had seen better days, and bought some rye bread and fresh vegetables.

If we had been grousing slightly about the wind up to now, we took it all back the next morning. We woke up to find the burgee pointing to home, and were outside the 'harbour' as soon as the flood tide started to slacken. Out came the Jenny as a spinnaker, and with the help of

the Elbe ebb we were soon ticking off the Elbe light-
ships. We held the spinnaker all through the night and
picked up Nordeney Lighthouse in the early hours. Later
in the afternoon we sailed gently passed the Borkumriff
Light vessel, and were close to Terschelling by the end of
the day. The wind was fitful, but always dead astern and
the nights were clear, with all the shore lights at around
maximum visibility. As we came round the corner to the
Texel we ran into much heavier traffic, and had to be
constantly on the alert to keep out of its way. The Texel
Light Vessel was giving us a good signal on the Seafix, and
was looming on the horizon as soon as the night came on.
The forecast was good, the wind was getting us along at
about 60 miles a day even though at times it was very
light, and we still had some of our rye bread left, my
crew finding it uneatable. Any thoughts we had of
putting into the Texel were banished, and we began to
head for Harwich, taking back bearings on the Texel.
A day out from here the wind improved, and we held on
to the Jenny as long as we dared making up to five knots
with the wind dead astern. This was a bit too much for
our boom fittings, and the preventer stay holding it down
pulled the bowsprit chain plate clean out. We had to
manage without a spinnaker for the rest of the night, but
by the morning I worked out a dead reckoning and made
us only 24 miles from the Outer Gabbard. The wind
dropped and we set the spinnaker from the Port side.
The sea was calmer and *Privateer* was not rolling about
as she had been doing earlier. We were getting radio
signals from the Outer Gabbard, but could not get a fix
of any accuracy. By nightfall we picked up the Ship-
wash and at last knew exactly where we were. We were
now getting the benefit of a strong sea-breeze, and were
racing over the tide towards the Sunk; the wind took us

round the Gunfleet, up the Wallet and only started to fail when we were sitting off Clacton Pier at breakfast time. By midday we were hoisting our yellow flag in Brightlingsea. After two months away it seemed a good time to clean up *Privateer*'s bottom, so as soon as we had cleared Customs I put her on the scrubbing posts. We scrubbed and slept all day, then lay off in the roads as she floated. The next day we were back on our mooring at Tollesbury. It was the 29th of August, so we had made it with one day to spare. *Privateer* looked scruffy, with marks and patches all over her paintwork, but these were outward appearances and she was surely the better for the exercise.

I had matched my father's voyage all those years before and had found the Baltic the splendid cruising ground he said it was.

CHAPTER XIII

More Journeys to the Past

After the excitement of our voyage to the Baltic we got back to our old routine, and I suppose of all the places we visited the one we liked best and returned to most often was Pin Mill. I had first come there with my father, by road; we would walk along the saltings in the winter and look at all the boats laid up under their covers. Many of these were old friends, like *Chequers,* the barge yacht that regularly wintered here, and father's own old boat the *Nicolette.* Pin Mill is a place where you do bump into people and boats that you know, so I suppose it shouldn't have surprised me once when we were strolling along the foreshore to see a boat laid up in the saltings that had a familiar profile. Will and I argued with each other as we got nearer; she was, was not, slightly smaller than *Privateer* there were other differences, or not. Finally we came up with her and read her name— *Lillibulero,* one of the three sister-ships built together at Gostelow's yard. It was a strange sensation looking at a boat which was an identical twin, or rather triplet, yet in some ways was not exactly the same. Here in fact was *Privateer* as she had been when she left the yard in Boston. There was a substantial cabin top, but no dog-house, improving her looks, I think, though making life harder for the galley-slave; the cockpit was taken slightly further aft, and the mast was stepped on the hog and not

119

in a tabernacle like ours. We noticed that instead of rigging screws *Lillibulero* had U-bolts, such as you often see on the stay of a telegraph pole. She was painted black, which no doubt accounted for why I thought she was marginally smaller than *Privateer*.

Lillibulero, sister-ship, moored at Pin Mill.

After this inspection it took us no time to find out the name of the owner and ring him up. Archie Campbell lived close to Pin Mill, and we made a rendezvous in the Butt and Oyster. He had owned our sister-ship for twenty years and was well acquainted with her history. *Lillibulero* was a famous boat, made so by her first owner, Johnston who had written a classic book about her, *Building a Little Ship*. Johnston has given an account in his book of the whole process of buying completing and fitting out the *Lillibulero,* and gives a fine pen portrait of her builder, Alexander Gostelow. A striking figure, Gostelow's height was increased by his wearing of high-heeled boots. This was so that he could put up a foot as a dolly when nails were being rove. By placing his boot with expert care in exactly the right position, the nail would come through in the hollow between heel and sole, rather than being driven into the boot. He was afflicted with a severe cast of the eye, which seems in no way to have affected his skill as a shipwright, but was disconcerting for all who spoke with him. Speaking of eyes, all his boats were built by eye; when, in later years he had changed over to building yachts instead of smacks, he once remarked wonderingly of a small yacht that she 'looked just like the half-model'. Johnston records that whenever there was an argument, as for instance about the diameter of the mast, Gostelow would resort to mumbling incomprehensibly. If this failed to wear down the resistance of the owner, Gostelow just carried on regardless and did what he knew was best. 'Well, there we be' he would remark— a statement to which Johnston could find no answer. Two of these arguments between owner and builder were over the mast; Johnston wanted one a couple of feet longer than *Privateer*'s, and this he achieved; but he also wanted a stick of seven inches diameter at the hounds, against the five-and-a-half inches that was traditional, and this he did not.

Johnston argued about this and other things, but he obviously had a great regard for Gostelow's skill and judgment. He describes how Gostelow would be so absorbed with some problem that he would let his supper get cold on the table. An innovation that Johnston claims credit for was the use of U-bolts on the shrouds, which we had noticed on *Lillibulero* still in place forty years later. This was an economical bit of do-it-yourself at the time, but I am not sure it would now be cheaper than buying a galvanised turnbuckle. Among other items that Johnston considered necessary were a sea-anchor and a square-sail. I don't know if Johnston ever had a use for the sea-anchor, I once was tempted to buy one at an auction, but I have not yet been in a situation where I regretted passing that one up. As for the square-sail, that must have been a useful sail with a fair wind, and was not so unusual in those days.

We kept in touch with our sister-ship for a while, but unfortunately Archie Campbell had to move down to the West Country, and *Lillibulero* was sold to a Dutch owner.

Pin Mill was the scene of more than one encounter with the past. One weekend we had a particularly fast passage down the Wallet, had brought up to anchor in our usual place, downstream of all the moorings on the southern side of the channel, and got ashore to the Butt and Oyster before opening time. We were standing on the hard waiting for this to happen and in the course of our conversation I had said something like 'Oh, that was before I bought *Privateer*'. Hearing the name someone else, also waiting for the door to open, overheard this remark, and picked it up. This was Leslie Potter who had owned her in the 1950s. His story was this.

Leslie was in the Merchant Navy, and was a victim of a careless and damaging accident; he was working on deck when a hatch-cover being lifted by crane, slipped and fell on him. As a result of this accident he lost a fore-arm and one of his legs was amputated below the knee. Faced with the problem of how to earn a living, but also the recipient of some compensation money, Leslie gamely decided he would buy a boat and go in for chartering. Like two of the previous owners, he must have felt that *Privateer* was a steady and handy boat that he could manage despite his disabilities, and this proved to be the case. He bought her and chartered her for two successful seasons. The first year he had sailed to the Baltic, as far as Finland, with a party of three; and he had taken the same party across the Bay of Biscay and to Genoa the next year.

It was Leslie who had made most of the changes which distinguished *Privateer* from *Lillibulero;* it was he who had put a turtle-back ply top on the cabin and added the doghouse; and it was he who had set the mast in a tabernacle on deck. This arose from his chartering, as he had intended to take parties on the Broads, and this means passing under the bridge at Oulton. He had also reduced the size of the mainsail and installed roller-reefing. Our main still carried the reef points like an appendix that was no longer of any use. Also we could see that the angle of the boom had been altered to clear the doghouse. All this reduced *Privateer*'s sail area, but has made her a handier boat. With his disabilities it was important for Leslie to avoid reefing if he could. Leslie had also replaced the ancient Kelvin two-cylinder engine with the Vedette. This was a second hand engine when he installed it, but a lot newer then than it was in our day. Of course we had carried Leslie off aboard, and this was the first time he had been on *Privateer* since he sold her and was in many ways a painful and sad experience for him. He told us the story which had led to him having to give up the idea of chartering and part with *Privateer*. Apparently there had been some mishap which involved an insurance claim. When the assessor came round he saw Leslie's disabilities and notwithstanding his record of successful cruising over the past two years, the insurance company refused to renew his cover. In spite of these sad memories, I am sure that Leslie was glad of the chance to tell the story and share it with us. On our side, we had put in place another piece of the jig-saw that was *Privateer*'s history.

CHAPTER XIV

Wardrobe

The sails that we inherited with *Privateer* had seen better days. When Leslie Potter had put in the doghouse he had cut down the mainsail so that it would fit the new arrangement, and he had also put on a roller-reefing gear. But the old reef-points were still hanging forlornly on the mainsail, now at an odd angle to the boom. This sail, though patched here and there, still had quite a few years of life in it, and it was only when we had decided to go to the Baltic that we thought we must replace it, so as not to be caught without a mainsail so far from home. The jibs—all three of them—were showing their age. The staysail, however, was the first to give out on us; it has a worse time than the other sails, flogs around when you come about and gets left without a cover over it. Unlike the jibs, which share the work between them, it is in use the whole time. We took the remnants of the old staysail along to Taylor's sail loft in Maldon and enquired about a new one. Old Mr Taylor reached for his folio behind the desk and flipped through the pages. 'Here's the one I made last time,' he said, pointing to a design-sketch which was dated 1953. 'Do you want the same again?' We did, and asked for the heaviest flax. We tried to put off the evil day when the jibs too would need replacing. We carried with us several sailmaker's palms, numerous needles and some of the purple bags the Post Office used for parcels. After a blow there would quite likely be a sewing party down below and the jibs acquired more purple patches. They blew one by one, the big Number One jib most spectacularly while sailing into Poole harbour close hauled in a force 6. Early on I had bought an old Genoa from one of the Burnham sailmakers. The luff was about thirty feet, so it would hoist from the end of the bowsprit to the masthead, but the clew then drooped down almost to the waterline by her chain plates. This sail made a very useful spinnaker set out on a fourteen foot pole, and being nylon it caught the lightest airs. As a headsail it was less useful, and though good on a broad reach it used to blow her head off the wind when closehauled. Replacing the jibs as our economy allowed, we had started with the storm jib, a pocket handkerchief of a sail which did at least balance her and made it possible to sail to windward. Without a jib at all *Privateer* is very badly behaved. With a lot of wind she is a handful to steer, and without it she makes very poor progress indeed. One time when I was crossing the estuary from Dover the bowsprit pulled out the gammon iron and in came the bowsprit and the jib; it took me three days to get back home across the estuary and the relief was considerable when I finally put her stem round the Swin spitway and eased the sheets after all that endless tacking.

We got our new Number One in time for the Baltic, and looked very grand for a while with a brand new white main and white jib. Mr Taylor had told me to leave the sails for one season to let the size wash out of them before tanning them with Canvo. All of these sails are of varying thicknesses of flax canvas, but heaviest of all is the trysail, a leg of mutton which we have rarely used. As with the others, old Mr Taylor found a drawing for this in his book, although Dr Dixon had finally changed his mind and decided to do without. There was one year when we came back from the West Country with the wind astern under trysail and staysail and made it from Owers to Beachy Head in seven hours, according to my log. With this stern wind there was no anxiety about a jibe, as we set the trysail without using the boom and let it drape itself against the after shroud. It is more of a piece of safety equipment than a working sail and I am not sure if Dr Dixon was wrong about it. Maybe one day I shall be glad of it.

That is really the whole story of our wardrobe, although we do think about topsails occasionally. Once I even found an old dinghy sail tiny enough to fit in the space between our yard and topmast; it made a surprising difference to our speed in light airs. Now that my children are all grown up and no longer regular crew, Pat and I often sail just the two of us; and we can probably do without the extra work involved in having a proper topsail. *Privateer,* let's face it, is undercanvassed and I prefer her that way. She will never win the Old Gaffers Race, but she is so snug-rigged that there is really never a need to reef her. Since reefing is always done in difficult conditions, it is often a cause of damage and disaster. It is easy to tear a sail while trying to put a reef in, and it takes two or even three to make a comfortable job of winding on a reef properly. I am often grateful that other people have to do this and I do not; whereas the only time I regret our small sail area is the last Saturday in July every year—the OG East Coast Race.

Privateer's famous sister-ship, the *Lillibulero* had a square sail and yard when she was first commissioned, but these are nowadays unusual. There was one yacht in the Crouch at Burnham with a squaresail yard a-cock bill when I was up that way recently, but the only other square sails I have seen are in the pictures on the wall inside the Kings Head in Tollesbury.

Flax canvas sails are so obviously appropriate for *Privateer* that there seems no need for any justification for them. Of course they cost less than nylon, or used to, and their life expectancy, judging by the dates in Mr Taylor's book seems to be about twenty years, except for the staysail: that seems to last a mere twelve years, but I think if I treat the current one with more care I can do better than this.

CHAPTER XV

Spars

When I bought her, *Privateer* had all her original spars. The mast was Swedish spruce, a beautiful bit of wood with not a rive in the whole length of it. There was a lot of bend in it, and the top-mast would curve round alarmingly under the weight of our masthead 'spinnaker'. We lost the bowsprit in the Tug-harbour at the Hook, so this was the first spar that had to be replaced. I had heard stories about the forester at Tangham forest—his telephone is on Orford exchange—and it seemed altogether a good idea to get a bowsprit from him. For a pound or two I drove over and collected eighteen feet of pine tree. I invested in a drawing knife and started work to whittle this down to a size that would go through the gammon iron and fit between the bits. This log was set up on board as we lay in the mud berth at Tollesbury (known locally as Rotten Row) and every tide that came in floated off the heaps of shavings and spread them around the creek. There was still a fringe of them along high water mark at the end of the season. My shoulders suffered horribly to begin with, and none of my coats fitted any more. The result never looked very smooth or professional, but it certainly seemed immensely strong, and was less inclined to bend than the old one.

This fine new sprit was not destined to last for long. On the way back from the West Country the next year, we had put in to Rye to leave *Privateer* for a week. The harbour master had lassoed her mast and secured it to the staithe—an arrangement I did not like, but I deferred to his local knowledge. When we came back the next Saturday, we found *Privateer* a sorry sight. The bowsprit had tucked itself under the dickerwork of the staithe at low tide, and was caught as the tide rose. At that time *Privateer* had a bowsprit stay, complete with turnbuckle, from the masthead to the cranch iron, so that the bowsprit had bent and pulled on the top of the mast, which snapped off at the hounds. Soon after, we were told, there was an almighty crack as the bowsprit itself broke off. We could hoist the 'Genoa', by its clew, and this did help to get us round the corner and into Ramsgate. But it was the engine that really brought us home, and it is under that heading that the story of that passage must be told. It seemed logical to go back to Orford again for a tree for our new mast, and Mr Jones the forester promised to look out a good one for me. It was an odd experience going back to these pine woods, as I remembered well the excitement when they were first planted. This had all been wild heathland, overgrown with bracken, and the men who were clearing it used to allow me to use the blow torch to set fire to the bracken. Over the years I had watched the little Christmas trees grow until now they were big enough to supply me with a mast. The tree was chosen, a lorry dropped it off at Tollesbury and Des Drake and Mouse got to work on it and turned it into a perfect replica of the original spar. Needless to say it was given endless coats of varnish before it was lowered into the tabernacle, and continued to have attention lavished on it thereafter. Des had followed the old tradition of painting it above the hounds, and very smart it looked. The old mast had been cut down to make our new bowsprit, and though this made it slightly on the big and heavy side, it is a fine spar and has carried our jib ever since. Incidentally, the top half of the mast also made itself useful; we had developed a nasty patch of rot in the boom where the after fitting bands it—a favourite place for trouble on a spar. Mouse spliced a bit of the topmast on to the after end of the boom, and this invisible mend has done us well ever since.

I wish I could say the same for the mast. Before using a Suffolk tree I had asked a fair section of expert opinion about this and no-one had advised against. But after a couple of years the spar began to show an undue number of rives. I kept filling these up with putty, but they opened up again, wider and longer. After only four years, a deep rive had started to rot, and while on holiday in Brittany I had knifed out a great gouge, low down, not much above the tabernacle. We knew that when we got home we should have to do something about this. In fact, we got blown off course on the way home, a strong North Easter headed us off into West Bay, and we were very glad to put into Exmouth. We ruled out bringing *Privateer* home to the East Coast that year, and so put her into the Exmouth canal at 'the Turf' a place we were to get to know very well that winter. The mast would obviously have to come down to be mended, and one day I unbent all the shrouds so as to make it ready to lower. During the night it blew hard, and the mast broke off at the tabernacle and fell on the tow path, fortunately doing no damage to our neighbours or to the pony that used to browse along the banks of the canal and that belonged to the Turf inn.

Although no-one told me this before, now everyone said that a tree raised in a warm area like Suffolk would never make a mast; the wood would always be soft and liable to rot—this being the historical reason why masts always came from Scandinavia, and English pine never used. Some people told me that I should have obtained a Scottish tree, and there were even those who claimed that the gentle climate of Wales would suffice. John Scarlett, the energetic secretary of the Old Gaffers Association, told me it would have been alright if I had soaked the tree in linseed oil for long enough. Meanwhile, as I was weighing up all this advice, *Privateer* sat in the Exeter canal with her rotten old mast lying broken on the towpath.

William, the younger of my two boys, now came into his own. When he left school he had gone straight round to Arthur Holt at Heybridge Basin and asked for a job as an apprentice. Arthur had not been going long at that time, he had built the remarkable twenty-eight footer the *Harnser* and was currently building the *Martha Kathleen*. If Arthur was not the only builder of wooden boats on the whole East Coast, he certainly was the only one we knew about. Will had not bargained about his pay, but after the first day or so, Arthur had agreed to pay him the normal apprentice wage. Will had been working on spars a bit and it was he that first spotted that one or two of the smacks on the Blackwater had used telegraph poles for masts. I followed this up and got an address in Braintree, which was where the Electricity Board had its depot. I spoke to them on the phone, and then drove over to Braintree, armed with a piece of chalk and a saw. At the depot I was told to go and find a pole from a heap over in the corner, where there lay a great pile of old poles, weathered, full of staples and bits of barbed wire. At the bottom of the heap was one which was smaller than the rest, about 34 feet long, and which was clearly unused. Close examination showed that one end was damaged, which explained why it was on the scrap heap with the others. I went back to the office and told them I had found one, but that it was at the bottom of the pile; could they help me get it out from under? 'That's your problem,' they replied—'You get it out.' I borrowed a crowbar and prised a pole on the top of the heap; with a bit of persuasion it rolled down and crashed to the ground. I worked away at the others until the neat heap was now sprawled all over the place and 'my' pole was exposed. It was in mint condition, the damage was at the extreme end, and that still left—comfortably—the 31 feet I needed. I set to work with the saw and an hour or so later I had removed the damaged end bit. I wrote my name all over the pole in chalk and went back to report to the office. The man was as emphatic as ever; 'thirty-one feet, that's eight metres, that's fifty pence a metre, thats *four pounds*'. I still have the receipt for this £4, item One Redundant Pole.

At that time my office was in a decaying warehouse on the Isle of Dogs, which we shared with a furniture store. I bribed the driver of a pantechnicon to pick up our pole and he was able to persuade some friendly lorry drivers on the site to load it up with their cranes. Parked outside our warehouse it looked a lot bigger than it had done earlier; it was a massive tree. At the base it measured 14" diameter, and this we had to reduce to six inches.

Will by this time had some experience of making spars, and he supervised the work. We hired a hand-held electric saw for the day, and made a series of cuts round the pole every six inches. Every two feet we changed the setting according to a table we had worked out previously. William had an adze of his own, and we borrowed another from a friend of his, and started to chip down until the grooves made by the saw were just visible. Then we planed away and finally hired a sander for the day to smooth it off. At this point we were half way

Starting work on the new spar.

through the job. The pole was far too thick to do the whole operation in one, we had to repeat the whole process, starting with the circular sawing. For some reason we had miscalculated our measurements on the first round, so that we had to up-end the spar, so to speak, to get it right the second time. Later I heard that the best spars were all upside down, so we could pretend we had done this on purpose. We checked our settings more carefully this time, knowing that anything we did was final. Our calculations were in fact right, but the saw we hired was not and had a tendency to slip; there are some grooves in the mast to show where this happened. On the adzing we were given some enthusiastic help— perhaps provoked by my own excessive caution with this tool. That has left a few scars as well. But despite these blemishes we finished with a fine looking spar; the creosote had penetrated right through to what is now the outside of the mast, so that it is a dark stained colour at the foot, but where it tapers above the hounds it is lighter in colour.

Although there was a lot of work on the new mast, the only part which I found really hard was shaping it and fitting the old hounds in the right place. In the end I got this wrong by about an inch, and we had to put a pad under the mast or the rigging would never tighten up. Another lorry driver was found going to Exeter and, packed up in sacking wraps, the new spar went down to be dropped near the Exeter end of the canal. Our Sport-yak dinghy made a fine pontoon and it duly floated down the canal, through the double lock and down to *Privateer*. The process had taken the entire winter.

While we lay in the Turf waiting for this to complete, we had decided to smarten up the other spars, so we plugged into the electric mains and took the paint off our boom and yardarm. We also incidentally took the paint off the cabin top and varnished that as well. It was all part of that process of smartening up *Privateer* for which I hold Pat mainly to blame.

Hoisting the finished spar in the Exeter Canal.

CHAPTER XVI

Repairs

When I became *Privateer*'s caretaker, on New Year's day 1966, the survey had shown only one patch of rot, and that was in the covering board and top-strake, where the rainwater had worked its way down the sides of one of the stanchions. Mr Frost of Frost & Drake had dealt with that and scarfed in a new section of shelf as well as a new piece of covering board and top strake. However, this did not stop all the other stanchions with their square entry through the covering board, doing their best to let rainwater through and cause trouble. However carefully you fill up the four-sided crack with pitch or whatever, as soon as the boat is sailing her hull begins to work, and loosens the join. I got used to this, and regularly gouged out bits of offending plank before the rot could spread. The top strakes, unlike the rest of the planking were of oak, but this did not stop these small patches spreading down wherever the stanchions had eased a gap. Below the waterline, we had no trouble at all, and in sixteen years we have found only one spot on the garboard which needed a graving piece fitting in. Gostelow was reported to have treated the planking of the boats he built with some anti-rot fluid; I think this must be true, and whatever it was it has been very effective.

The decks needed recaulking, and the first time this arose I got Des Drake to do it; but after that I kept up a sort of continual recaulking wherever it was needed. Again this seemed to me like an insoluble problem; whenever there was a prolonged dry spell the deck planking would shrink away from the pitch and open up the seams. For many years we put up with this, pouring more of a variety of gunjes into the seams, and trying to arrange that our sleeping faces were not immediately below a drip. After about five or six years of this fairly happy-go-lucky existence we were in for a nasty shock. Right up in the tuck at the after end of her counter there was widespread rot. There were two things I should have done to prevent this, and which I had failed to do, never having got round to it. One was to pour ladles of pitch at the after end until it filled up all the angles of the frames where water could stand. When each little nook was full, the pitch would run down and fill the next and so on. This was the recommended way with smacks, I had been told to do it but was now paying for the omission. The other recommendation, which I followed too late, was to put a couple of ventilators into the deck over the tuck to ensure that the air circulated around this enclosed and inaccessible space. In *Privateer* the tuck was even more blocked off than it might have been as there was a large cooling box in the last section of the exhaust, well and truly barring access.

Chris was luckily at a loose end at about this time, and he was put in charge of what turned out to be a major operation. We put *Privateer* into Heybridge Basin and took off the deck aft of the cockpit. It was a pretty horrid sight. The chocks, solid pieces of oak that supported the after end of the deck planks were water-logged. The rot had affected the stanchions and some bits of deck beam. During the spring Chris worked away at this very awkward job; the particular difficulty was that each of these chocks had to be shaped exactly in every dimension to fit in place against the frames and hull planking and give the exact flat surface for the deck planks on top. Even Watts & Jurd, the boatbuilders' bible, accustomed as it is to describing processes of great complexity, refers to chocks as 'very intricate'. It is no exaggeration, they have to fit in so many dimensions at once, and stay in place when spiked to the frame ends. The operation was master-minded by Dilbury Clarke, who directed Chris in every move from his shed by the canal bank.

Dilbury had been a barge skipper, and was still retained by the owner of the *Edith May,* which lay in the basin just by his shed. Dilbury was a skilled and experienced shipwright who was generous as very few craftsmen can be with his time and advice, and also in lending his tools, which is even more unusual. Chris would take along a chock and explain the problem, and Dilbury would recommend the best method and maybe lend a prized gouging chisel, then Chris would go back and follow instructions until the next stage was reached. All this while Dilbury made it a point of principle never to step aboard. I never found out whether the reason for this (which would have saved a lot of time in explanations as *Privateer* was berthed almost directly opposite his shed) was because he was paid a retainer to look after the barge *Edith May* and felt that he should not be seen aboard any other craft, or whether he thought his teaching methods would be less effective if he got too closely involved with the job in hand. I hoped that no-one took advantage of Dilbury's extreme generosity, though I fear that some of his priceless collection of tools were never returned.

Dilbury used to hold court every lunch time at the door of his shed, and every now and then there would be a ripple of laughter from his audience as he told some anecdote. He was a born raconteur and his judgments on people could be very shrewd and sometimes surprisingly sharp.

The timber yard at Heybridge looked through their sheds and found us a piece of Canadian spruce, which they planed for the seams, and Chris went on a successful hunt for some oak, which I think in the end was contributed by a pensioner who had recently had a window taken out of his house and led us to the old frame. He had once worked for Sadds and knew a bit of good wood when he saw one, and had been watching Chris's patient progress with an interested eye. I found a couple of brass ventilators going cheap at Dixon Kerley's in Maldon, and when these were fitted the job was at last complete. We have had no more trouble from that end.

Some years later Will had his turn on the bow. Coming round the North Foreland, always a rough patch of water, the shackle holding the bobstay to the stem had parted; the jib now pulled the bowsprit upwards and wrenched out the gammon iron, with some damage to the deck planking. We replaced the bitts and also the pad under the bowsprit. The old oak had gone soft underneath where rainwater had found its way, and we replaced it with a splendid piece of solid hardwood that Will had found as driftwood on the seawall.

Apart from these incidents, it was routine payeing of the deck seams, the endless battle against small leaks in the decks, and the problem of the stanchions where they came through the covering board. Everyone knows that the best protection against rot is plenty of sailing, and this treatment was on the whole successful.

CHAPTER XVII

Brittany

For the first ten years we had cruised *Privateer* we had invariably turned left at Dover, either to follow the French coast down towards Normandy, or more often to make for Belgium, Holland, or, once, the Baltic. During all these wanderings, alongside old or new friends in endless harbour talks, the subject of Brittany often came up. It was the most beautiful cruising ground to be found anywhere, the dangers of the rocky coastline were greatly exaggerated, and so on. I read some of the books and listened, but in the end always decided that *Privateer* should not be exposed to the risks. There was some logic to this as well as illogic. On the East Coast, the tides run parallel with the sandbanks, so that a boat with no engine power available will not drift onto a hazard. There is holding ground between the shoals, and in the last resort if you do miscalculate and go aground, it is on hard sand at the worst, not rock. A glance at a chart of the Brittany coast shows that none of these factors apply; the tides run very hard indeed athwart the channels, and so would sweep a boat on to the rocks; much of the area is too deep for anchoring. One of my friends, Dick Oxby, who used to urge me to go to Brittany had put his own boat, the *Polly Peachum* on to a pinnacle of rock. Michael Miller had lost the lovely old *Quiver* between Roches Douvres and Sept Isles. Perhaps

141

the urging of Fred Lockwood who had taken *Patna* there the previous year, perhaps because our trip to the Baltic had exhausted that direction and left us no option, or maybe we had grown more confident with the years—whatever the reason, I got hold of the Brittany *Pilot* and bought some charts; the next year we would turn right at Dover.

With Pat and William for crew, we set off harbour-hopping, putting in to Shoreham and the Solent, all places to which we had never taken *Privateer*. We needed to get into Yarmouth, where we were to pick up Chris, and I tried to do this by beating through the harbour entrance. A ferry was alongside and this reduced the width of the entrance to about twenty yards at most. Since our length, with bowsprit, is 45 feet this did not work out, and we had to drop the hook hurriedly and then try to get the engine going. We were able to make up for this the next day by sailing *out* of the harbour. We were carried, largely by the ebb tide rather than by the air of wind, down past the Needles and in through the entrance to Poole, this time with the indispensible assistance of the flood tide. Off Brownsea Island I made a bad miscalculation; we had a four weeks' growth on the bottom and I wanted to scrub off as much as possible before crossing the channel. The rise and fall was only about four feet, which made it just possible—but I was caught by an outlying shoal where we were stuck in soft mud and only showed a few inches of weed at low water. We would have to take our barnacles for a Brittany holiday with us.

We left the next day with a fair wind, but very light, and made an average of only 2 knots on course for Cherbourg, even with the Genoa doing its best as a spinnaker. After ghosting along all day, we listened to

the six o'clock forecast, which gave us force 7 or gale.
Down came the spinnaker, we changed to Number Three
jib and battened down the forward hatch. The wind had
not heard the forecast, and disappeared altogether, so
that we spent the whole night drifting up and down with
the tide. The next morning a very light air got up, but the
tide was now setting westerly and there was no way we
could make Cherbourg. We altered course for Alderney,
but the tide triangle on the chart was a very odd shape,
with our speed of about 2 knots and the tide doing nearly
twice as much. Keeping a steady bearing on Alderney was
none too easy, as we could see that any slight error
would carry us either into the Alderney Race, or past the
island to the North. The Genoa drew well, it was a fine
day with good visibility, and we could see the Braye
harbour breakwater very clearly. We sailed in and
dropped anchor inside the harbour. Even in these calm
settled conditions we were pitching a bit inside and we
could imagine what it would be like in any sort of a
blow.

I had passed Alderney often enough in the remote
past, and viewed its rather stark profile from a distance,
but never been ashore before. The little village and main
street is straight out of the 19th century, while the
extensive ruins of German fortifications are a reminder
of a less cosy past.

In the morning there were signs of more breeze, and
we laid a kedge, tripped our anchor and sailed the kedge
out, tacking out of the entrance to Braye and past the
submerged extension of the breakwater. With wind
astern we set course for Guernsey's northern entrance,
through the Little Russell channel and hardly noticed
that we were being carried through the dreaded Race. By
lunch time we were in St Peter Port harbour and secured

to a buoy. It is a restless harbour, with much coming and going and occasional violent rolling. Also it can take you by surprise—though not on this occasion—by drying out completely. We were not entirely sorry to be off early the next morning, in very bad visibility. We were making three or four knots into the fog, and getting bearings on the Roches Douvres Radio Beacon. At last we sighted the Lighthouse, and I thought it would be prudent to pass it on the East side, although this meant fighting the west-going tide. This was probably unnecessary on my part, but I didn't want to tangle with the tail of outlying rocks on the west of the group, and I wanted to keep the lighthouse in sight as long as possible. An hour later we had passed the Roches Douvres and were setting course for Barnouic. This is only five or six miles past the Roches Douvres, and its top appeared above the mist in roughly the right place. We worked past Barnouic, by now with an easterly tide setting strongly, and manouvred to get it dead astern on the new course so that we could take back bearings and check our course. We were now aiming for Horaine tower, and making a good four knots through the water. But the visibility had not improved with the wind, and was down to less than a mile. Dead astern of us I saw a glimmer of white which I first thought was the sun shining on the top of Barnouic, but later showed itself as a white sail coming up on us. This yacht was followed by two more, all gaining on us fast. At least we were all pointing the same way—unless that is, they were rashly following us. We were taking back bearings by Seafix on Roches Douvres, but this was now too far astern to give us an accurate position. There was still no sign of Horaine. The leading yacht came up with us and immediately executed a turn to starboard; there up to the north west was a lighthouse,

and closer to us a buoy. We held close to the yacht and
followed her, and by doing so failed to close and read
the buoy, which in the mist I had wrongly identified as
black and white. This error threw me completely, and
I began to hunt for the black and white buoy on the
map. In fact we had slightly overshot and were a mile or
so to the eastward of Horaine, but I was so badly dis-
orientated by the business of the buoy that I failed to
identify Horaine, which was unmistakeable really. While
I was fiddling about with this problem the two other
yachts overhauled us, and we now faced a new quandary.
Two yachts were passing the tower and going on to the
West, but the third, and nearest, made an abrupt turn to
port and steered in towards the land. After an agonised
hesitation I followed. We had now at all costs to keep this
yacht in sight or we were completely lost, and in fact the
white sails of the yacht about half a mile ahead were the
only visible object. We trimmed the sheets and tried to
get all the speed we could out of *Privateer,* while Chris
fastened his eyes on the sail ahead determined not to
lose it. We kept on like this for twenty very long minutes
—it still makes me shiver to think of them—just holding
on to the tail of the yacht ahead, before at long last we
picked up a red and white buoy to starboard, and almost
at the same moment, the grey outline of land behind it.
This was, could only be, the Isle de Bréhat, and now that
we were back on the map again, we began to pick up
identifiable marks all over the place.

Our troubles were not entirely over; what had happened was this. We had intended to follow the main entrance
into the Pontrieux river, which was the route taken by
the leading two yachts. We had followed a short cut
round the wrong side of Ile Bréhat which is a narrow and
rock-strewn high-water channel. However, by the time we

had identified Men Garo, a rock marked by a beacon, the mist was clearing and we could see beacons clearly on either side of the *rade*. All were prominently named in red and white paint, and the rocks seemed less intimidating with their friendly name-tags. We were quickly in behind Bréhat and could see the main channel of the Pontrieux river ahead of us. By seven-thirty we had passed the little fishing village of Loguivy and found ourselves an anchorage in six fathoms. It had seemed like a long day.

The next morning we wondered why we had ever made a fuss about coming to Brittany. The sun was shining, we were in a river with steep wooded slopes which was quite the most beautiful place we had ever sailed to; all the rocks were painted in gay colours with their names clearly spelt out. We got used to paying out shackles of cable that we had rarely seen before, sometimes to the bitter end. With a rise and fall of thirty-six feet, the minimum amount of chain had to be over twenty fathoms. We explored Bréhat, we found a good beach at Loguivy and lay there to scrub off—no problem here like there was in Poole! The Bretons were very friendly, especially when they established that we had not come over to fish in their waters. We went up river as far as we could, to Lézardrieux. Here we had a pleasant surprise one morning.

We had anchored the previous night off the town and woke to find ourselves hidden in a thick mist. As it slowly cleared we saw what at first appeared to be a mirage; quite close to us was a mirror-image of *Privateer*. As the mist cleared we could see that she was bigger, and in fact was the *Rhoda Gostelow*, a lovely yacht built in 1938 and beautifully maintained; there was no mistaking the family resemblance. The extra few feet makes a lot of difference—down below, for instance, there was sitting headroom under the decks; and she carried a main that was huge compared to ours. I think my eye roved ever so slightly, for the first and only time.

Having once broken the taboo on Brittany, we came again, the very next year. We followed a route down the French coast, across the Normandy Bay and to the next door river up to the old cathedral town of Treguier. This time we had no trouble with fog making our landfall and picked up the Lighthouse Les Heaux. But we ran into very nasty fog on the way back, and got into St Peter Port only with the help of our Seafix.

I had tried to come in through the Northern entrance—the Little Russell channel—in very thick fog, hoping that I would pick up the foghorn on Fougière and come in on that. I had come in as close as I dared but heard no foghorn, so decided to work my way all round the west coast of Guernsey and come in by the more straight-forward southern channel. The fog was so thick there was no point in keeping a look out and I spent almost the entire night down below getting fixes on the Casquets and the Guernsey Beacon, and drawing tide triangles. On the Northwest corner of Guernsey we had a very nasty moment when we heard the sound of breaking water on our *sea*ward side. You can imagine I took check after check on all available lines on the chart, while the sound got nearer and louder. Only when it reached us did I realise that it was the ebb tide coming up on us—I've not met such a noisy tide anywhere else. For twenty minutes it lapped and hissed round us, then passed on ahead. We edged our way round the corner and into the wide entrance just as dawn was breaking, and with it gaps in the fogbank. We were relieved to say the least when we finally secured in St Peter Port, and went ashore

to buy some spare batteries for the Seafix. We also looked
wistfully at a Patent log in the window of the chandlers.
During that night I had been using running fixes
consistently—the Casquets were too far away for
sufficient accuracy, and would have found this a lot
easier if I had had a better idea of the distance
travelled.

On our way back from Brittany we found ourselves
stuck for the winter in the Exeter canal; and this gave us
the chance to explore Brixham and Dartmouth—the latter
a place where we found many old gaffers and a friendly
welcome. Brixham was rather a disappointment from my
recollections of it as a child when it was full up with
Brixham trawlers. We also spent some time at Emsworth
on the way back, where again we had a very hospitable
reception. The two places we felt most at home along this
coast, Emsworth and the Exe, both have certain
similarities with the East Coast and 'the Turf' at the
beginning of the Exeter canal is not unlike Heybridge
Basin, with its small community of do-it-yourself yachtsmen. In here we met the owner of a three-masted ocean
going schooner, as we thought a copy of the famous
Vendredi Treize except that she was built a year or two
earlier. We also found two brothers doing up an old
smack, one of whom left a portrait of *Privateer* in our
cabin the day we locked out.*

* It is reproduced in the end-papers.

CHAPTER XVIII

Missing Link

Privateer had been in my care for sixteen years, and I felt I knew her ways fairly well. I could tell when the first barnacle growth on her hull was beginning to slow her down, I knew what it felt like when she got the bit between her teeth in a force five or six and raced through the water with the dinghy planing astern like a speed boat. I knew how badly she would roll when she was becalmed at sea, and what an awful rattling of blocks there was. And I knew the gentle conversational noises she made when sailing the sea with a light breeze. I also knew most of her history. In Dover once I entertained a man who had sailed in her in the 'fifties and who told us that the owner then was a Thames pilot who kept her at Gravesend for a while. In Maldon Jack Feesey had told us about Dr Dixon, who had kept her at the yard there and finally sold her to Pike and Jarman when he emigrated to Australia. (Dr Dixon was another of *Privateer*'s owners with a handicap, in his case he was missing an arm.) *Building a Little Ship* told us quite a bit about Gostelow her builder, but there was still this gap over the first three years. This gap was to be filled in more detail than we could ever have hoped.

Once again it was at Pin Mill; this time I was sheltering there under the lee of the hanging wood and waiting for some extremely wet and windy weather to pass over. Pat and I were in the chandlery there, nosing around for something to take back aboard and read, when Pat picked up the current issue of *Coast & Country,* a journal which is now, alas, extinct. Flipping through it idly, she came on a picture which brought her up short; without the doghouse, with a flatter cabin top it was still unmistakeably *Privateer*. The snap was of her lying in Brixham, but the accompanying article was an account of her maiden voyage, from Boston, in March 1932. It was written not by her owner, but by Rex Pasley who had volunteered to skipper her on this delivery voyage. Rex has told the story himself, and no-one could tell it better, so the whole story is printed in the Appendix. I have always kept well away from that part of the world myself, considering the North Norfolk coast and the Wash to be a dangerous area, and this maiden voyage was certainly hazardous. It was fortunate that Rex was obviously a fine seaman and came out of the exploit unscathed. Ironically, they finished up not in the Crouch, where they were heading, but in Orford, where *Privateer* lay from March until August of that year. The story had involved the Cromer lifeboat and the famous Coxswain Blogg and had got into the local paper. I must have rowed our dinghy and sailed the *Sylvia* many times past *Privateer* as she swung to her anchor that year, but I don't remember her and I don't recall any echo of that story, quite enough of an incident to merit being passed around and handled by the sailing community at Orford.

As soon as we had read this account, of course we made it our business to get in touch with its author, Mr Pasley. Inland, far from the sea, I found Rex, a small, neat man nearly ninety years old, his house full of models he had made and mementoes of his sailing days. He was delighted to meet *Privateer*'s current owner and treated Pat and me with great kindness and generosity. He handed over to our keeping the original log of that first voyage, beautifully kept in his copperplate handwriting and meticulously detailed on weather conditions and states of the tide. He also gave us some photos taken at that time. *Privateer* was an especially pleasant memory for him, as he and his wife had done their first cruising together in her. What had happened was this. The owner, Kemlo, after his unpleasant experience of the first voyage, had handed *Privateer* over to Rex who had sailed her as if she were his own boat for three years. He and his wife sailed her that first year over to the Swale; the next year, 1933, up to Brancaster and then over to Flushing. In 1934 they cruised down the south coast and as far as Brixham, where the photo we had seen had been taken. All these passages were recorded in Rex's log, which he had passed on to me. By that time Rex was ready to take delivery of his own boat, the *Fortisan* and surrendered *Privateer* to her owner. But Kemlo had other plans, and sold her to build another boat, the *Bird of Dawning.* Above the waterline the two boats are not so dissimilar, both being traditional gaff cutters, but I have seen *Bird of Dawning* out of the water and her hull is not that of a smack but of a yacht, with a deep keel which gives her a very different performance to windward. *Privateer* had been sold to a Mr Herbert, who installed her first engine (Rex had done all his cruising without one) and immediately sold her to Mr Whitworth, the schoolmaster with a wooden leg. Before doing so Herbert had done something for which I am in his debt; he had caused various carvings to be made on the beams: on the main beam, '4.24 registered tonnage', inside the after locker, 'Bo'suns store .25 tons' and in the foc'sle, 'Chart Space 1.25 tons'. In other words he had fulfilled the conditions of the

Rex Pasley crossing West Bay,
1935.

Merchant Shipping Act and registered *Privateer*. From
this Certificate of Registry, duly filled in on every change
of ownership, I was later able to trace *Privateer*'s later
history; the first three years I had been given at first hand

by Rex Pasley. After our visit, I had written to thank him for his hospitality, and the answer came not from him but from Mrs Pasley. He had died suddenly after going out to do some gardening, I am sure he was glad to hear news of *Privateer* before he died, and I often think of him and how he saved her from pounding herself to pieces on the sand at Mundesley.

CHAPTER XIX

Iron Topsails

A fine weekend morning on the Blackwater; *Privateer* is heading downstream with a light breeze astern, at a guess giving us four knots through the water. Up from astern comes a modern four-berth yacht, sails furled and under power. Her engine gives her a slight edge on us and she slowly overtakes, then disappears gradually in the distant haze. I shall never understand why she is not using her sails. The situation will be familiar to everyone who frequents the coasts, and is only an extreme form of the question; should a sailing boat have an engine at all, and if she does, when should it be used?

When my father's boat *Uldra* was built in 1905 she had no engine; but a few years later, in 1912 an engine was installed; without any question it was more trouble than it was worth. So the debate was going on before 1914, and continued—with a wide range of engines being made—in the twenties and thirties. When *Privateer* was built she had no engine either, but four years later her second owner, who perhaps had only bought her as a speculation and may have felt that she would fetch a better price with an auxiliary, fitted her with a 2-cylinder Kelvin. The engine was nine years old at the time and was credited with 7½ H.P. and an ability to drive *Privateer* at 4 knots. The two rather bulky cylinders (about 700 cc each) stood up high and the whole engine was large and heavy—and slow running. But it had proved popular in the twenties with fishing boats and also as an auxiliary. I heard a yarn about this engine from old Mr Feesey, of Dan Webb and Feesey, who had gone up to Hull to fetch *Privateer* along with her then owner, probably in 1960. They were collecting her in February, and a northerly gale sprang up astern of them; somewhere past Lowestoft the following seas had begun to threaten to poop them, and a sea lifted the counter and started to pour through the exhaust. In no time the engine was full and there was water all over the cabin floor. This decided them to put in for Harwich, but they needed the engine to turn up the entrance, so Jack stopped the flow from the exhaust, drained the cylinder block and managed to get the engine going on one of its cylinders in time to make Harwich. It was soon after this incident that Leslie Potter replaced the Kelvin with a new—well, nearly new—Morris Vedette. In the '50s these along with the Ford 1000, were the normal choice for a fishing boat or smack auxiliary. They were certainly built to last, and thirty years later it was still possible to get spares, as I was to discover. This was the engine that I inherited, about sixteen years old as it then was. During the first two or three years I used the engine quite a bit, although this entailed a lot of time being spent cleaning plugs, blowing through jets and tapping gently at sticky valves. As I got more used to *Privateer* and her ways I gradually found I was using the engine less and less and doing without it became almost a principle. I got more satisfaction from beating up the narrow Tollesbury Fleet, judging when to round the boats moored in mid-stream, when to back the staysail, when to pinch shamelessly over the weather mud bank— then the final anguish over when to drop sails and stake everything on putting the bow close by the mooring

buoy—than in running up under power. Even more
satisfactory was to get the engine going for a warm-up
only when we were securely moored and didn't need it
any more; perverse, but on the whole I always felt more
secure when relying on sails than on the engine. All very
well while it was going, but if it took into its head to
stop when I was in the middle of a crowded anchorage
or trying to get into a pontoon harbour, as could happen,
then I was in worse trouble than I could ever be under
sail. I found I was usually listening to the throb of the
engine like an anxious doctor with a heart-patient, and all
too often with a missing heart-beat or a worrying change
in pulse rate. That old Vedette, however, performed
better than I deserved; despite neglect it managed as a
rule to come up to scratch and do what was needed. It
took us miles and miles through the Dutch canals once
with an obstruction in the pump which reduced the flow
of cooling water, so that we were blowing off steam
through the outlet. Every year the compression got a bit
worse, not that this worried me as far as speed was
concerned as we never expected it to do more than a
steady pull, but it did make starting more difficult. It
would no longer start on the handle and required the
electric starter, and this had so many defective contacts
that every other time I pushed the button nothing
happened and I had to dive down and get my finger and
thumb round the knob on the after end of the starter
and give it a quarter turn. This engine's finest hour was in
fact its swan song, when I made a passage under power,
the only time I have done such a thing.

This was after we had lost the top of our mast in Rye,
and had struggled round to Ramsgate. I was joined there
by Frank Mulville who offered to help get me home
across the estuary, and as the wind was completely absent

all day we did the whole passage under power. Every now and then the plugs got so hot that we had to stop and take them out to cool. A few minutes later we started up again and they would do another long stretch. I spent most of the time down below as apart from the plugs there was work to be done on the petrol supply. We had plenty with us but as I normally went in for rather short runs under power, my petrol tank was of 5-pint capacity, an old Seagull tank in fact. This was slung in the galley so that there was a good gravity feed down to the carburettor with no possibility of air-locks. It wasn't easy to get more than about three pints into the tank without risk of spillage, on the other hand I didn't want to run her dry, so I was kept pretty busy.

This trip was not made easier by a very thick fog which came down on us just as we were entering the Edinburgh channel. Frank steered a course and checked on the depths with the echo sounder while I (when not busy down below) went up forward to listen for ships' engines and act as lookout. We saw none of the buoys in the Edinburgh, but Frank followed the contours and quietly altered course. With visibility at twenty yards or so, I was straining my eyes forward to see anything— other craft, buoys, ships maybe—when a steel structure loomed out of the murk a few yards to starboard. I yelled back to Frank at the helm, and then realised what it was; we passed about thirty feet away from the Barrow Beacon that marks the southern end of the Barrow. Frank has taken to sailing single-handed with no-one to appreciate his landfalls, so I am glad he had a witness for that piece of navigation.

After the Barrow tower it was a straightforward run down to the Spitway, and the difficult bit now being over the mist began to clear. But the strain on the engine was beginning to tell; there were more and more missing heartbeats, and by the time we got safely back to our mooring, nearly twelve hours after our start from Rams-gate harbour, the old Vedette was down to two cylinders. There was a blessed silence as I switched it off; it was its last splutter and I was never able to get it to fire again.

The demise of this old Vedette was the signal for some very heady talk about its replacement. During the winter (1971/2) I visited the Boat Show and looked at what was available. I had a hankering for a diesel—a disease which affects a lot of owners of ageing petrol engines—and was particularly taken with the Japanese Yanmar, then newly on the market, and going for about £200-£250. I couldn't afford it, but there was no harm in looking. I got as far as mentioning this to the Tollesbury marine expert, Reg. I explained that I had a clapped out Vedette and what did Reg think about the idea of a diesel? Reg roused himself; how often did I use an engine anyway? what on earth did I want a diesel for? In any event a diesel would shake all the fastenings out of *Privateer* and finish her off. If this were not a conclusive argument, another one was; this was to do with the siting of the Vedette. The gearbox of the Vedette had a plate on its after end to which was bolted up the reduction-gear; this was offset about eight inches from the line of the crank shaft, below and to port, to connect up with the propeller shaft. It seemed that no other engine besides the Vedette had this offset reduction gear, and therefore no engine would fit up against the existing shaft. Expense ruled out without discussion putting in a new shaft, so there was only one thing to do; get another Vedette.

Once decided on this proved easy; the columns of Exchange and Mart were full of Vedettes in working order, and after an exchange of £75 and an impressive

dry run in a private garage I was again the owner of an
engine. Tom Hedgecock installed it in Heybridge basin
and took the old one away for spares.

In removing the old engine, the exhaust pipe had
crumbled in our hands; it was nothing more than a lot of
rust held together by an asbestos bandage. I had picked
up some copper piping cheap and thought to save what
I could in what was turning out to be an expensive year
by bending the exhaust pipe myself. I made an elaborate
model of its very erratic course from manifold to exhaust
box in the tuck, and set to work. First I filled the copper
tube with sand as I had been told that this would stop it
collapsing inwards when being bent. Then I made some
jigs for putting in the bends, and started to warm it up
with the burner. All I can pass on in the way of experience is that the way I put the sand in didn't stop it
collapsing, and I still have an odd-shaped length of
copper pipe lying around in the garage. Fortunately
there was enough over for Mr Hedgecock to do a more
professional job on it.

This engine, especially when newly installed, was
distinctly lively and was especially useful its first year in
the Dutch waterways and getting in and out of the small
Danish harbours of the Baltic. Like its predecessor it had
one or two foibles; it had a tendency to idle forward
when in neutral, and this made it very hard to slow down.
Privateer's ten tons carry a lot of way in any event, but
the gentle forward idling of the screw helped to keep her
going rather faster than required when coming alongside.
It may be asked—then why not put her astern when
coming to? This was the other foible; it was impossible
to get *Privateer* to go astern. If you held the gear lever
(or whatever was being used for one at the time) hard
back you could get some engagement astern, but as soon

as the engine was revved up she simply slipped and nothing happened. The moment I let go of the gear lever to throw a line or fend off, the forward idling would start up again. Several fine mechanics tried to remedy this defect, and at one time I thought that there must be some inherent reason why *Privateer* refused to go astern, but as long as we had a Vedette engine we could not cure her of this habit. We developed a whole range of braking systems whenever we found ourselves in the Dutch waterways or similar confined spaces; the absence of reverse did not bother us on our own shores. We used to carry the kedge ready to throw on a length of line, estimate the distance and then when we had come up against the lock gate or whatever, we would have to row back and recover the anchor. A better system was a small grapnel which we would throw to catch a stanchion on the canal bank, being careful that there were no lock-keeper's legs in the way. Where there were no stanchions we had a third method—the most expendable member of the crew would leap ashore with a line and dig in his heels. This reminds me, or the other way about perhaps, of the method used by the lighters in one of the German rivers, reported by that fine motor-boat voyager Pilkington. The lightermen would come down river with the weight of their craft giving them steerage way over the fast flowing river. When they wanted to bring up they would edge in to the bank and the crew would leap ashore with a sort of plough which he would quickly engage in the field alongside the river bank. The meadows alongside the river were full of these random, crooked and somewhat inconsequent plough marks, for all the world as if there had been a very drunken Drawing Match.

Although I did make efforts to maintain my second Vedette better than the first one, and went down to start

it through the winter, it began to suffer from the same
troubles as the old one. Over and over again we would
find ourselves warping into Heybridge basin, towing with
the dinghy, and then sailing out again if we could not get
a lucky snatch from a friendly yachtsman. I was always
hoping to amaze the lock-keeper, George Clarke, by going
in or out under my own steam, but this happened less
and less often. Going out of the lock there was usually
some help from the flow of the canal water running out
into the stream, but once this slewed us on to the mud to
the side of the scoured channel. George took this very
calmly, threw us a line and attached his end of it to the
electrically powered lock-gate; as it closed it pulled us
inch by inch off the mud, and this time we made sure to
keep to the channel. Going in can be more difficult, and
I remember once hovering at the entrance to the lock
while the canal stream worked against us. 'Hoist a bit of
rag!' shouted George, and we hastily put up the staysail;
a puff of wind funnelled up into the basin and carried us
gently with it.

I once had some sweeps for *Privateer,* and these were
very useful for a long row, and without the fuss of getting
out the dinghy, but all three of them, separately, disappeared and I have searched the foreshore in vain to find
a replacement. I have heard that the old Thames bargees
used to pole along the edge of the sandbanks when there
was no wind to propel them, and I have tried this with
what is known on board rather grandly as the 'spinnaker
boom'. This method is one I have not been able to master
and the bottom is either too uneven, as in coming up the
St Osyth shore to Brightlingsea, or too muddy and soft,
as with practically everywhere else.

So, it has been the dinghy that has served as the
normal means of propulsion when the wind fails. Un-

rivalled when it comes to entering a congested harbour, it has the ability to turn *Privateer* in her own length, lines can be taken to buoys, or ashore to take a quick turn round a bollard. Or slowly crossing the estuary, pulling past the Shivering Sand Fort at a steady speed of 1 knot; once I had to row for three hours in the North Sea to get clear of the shipping lanes. Rowing-and-towing takes you where you want to go, albeit slowly; but more than that it overcomes the awful impatience which seizes the becalmed sailor and enrages him.

Gradually the 'new' Vedette slipped into the ways of the old one. Refits became more frequent, the compression got worse. One day coming up the creek at low water with a head wind it suddenly stopped, never to start again. This was shortly before we had planned to break an old taboo and cruise to the Somme estuary; I sailed up to Maldon twice to try to get expert help, but nothing would persuade it to go. Once more we had to face the problem of a clapped out engine.

We spent the first day of our holiday taking the head off the engine and putting in a new gasket. It was almost a relief when that made no difference; now we could get on and enjoy our holiday and forget about the engine and its endless ailments.

We crossed over to the Swale, and rather than risk entering Ramsgate under sail ran back to Harty Ferry. Here we lay on a buoy for three days while it blew a gale from the east. It took us an hour and a half to row ashore and as long to make the return trip. Less far off was a six-tonner anchored close in to Harty, and we made friends with the owner and his wife. They had just installed a one-cylinder Yanmar diesel, which everyone had said would be too small, but which turned out to be entirely adequate and thoroughly reliable. The owner had also built a boat years before at Gostelows, and it was he who told me about Alexander Gostelow's high-heeled boots.

By the time the wind had abated we gave up the idea of getting to France, and decided to sail round the back of Sheppey to the Medway—something we had never done. We found the Medway full of interesting creeks, and with plenty of room for us to anchor. We behaved as if we had a highly infectious disease, and tended to anchor well clear of all other boats, so as to allow for getting under way whatever the wind without getting tangled with the neighbours. We wondered why we had never been up the Medway before; we are not the only East Coast sailors who neglect the Medway. The upper reaches are a bit crowded, but we found a space to drop the anchor and take the dinghy up to Rochester. Lower down there are plenty of creeks and backwaters to explore, and we shall have to go back to find them all.

Sailing round the back of Sheppey was interesting, we did it at Low Water and found just enough water in the narrow channel. If we had had the use of the engine we might have turned up Milton Creek, but the entrance looked very narrow and we pressed on round the corner. Here the wind was heading us and the young flood was now of course against us too. As we tacked across we gained a few feet with each pair of boards, unless the wind played tricks and set us back a bit. After two hours of beating we had made a cable or so, passing the various ruined jetties and abandoned factories and brickworks that crowd the shore, and were getting near to the end of the reach. At last we were round and on a broad reach to the combined rail and road bridge. We blew our horn three times, hoisted a bucket in the shrouds and hoped the bridge keeper would understand that we had no power. (Surely there should be a signal hoist for this?). At last there were signs of opening, but by now there were four or five other craft circling around; I tried to time it like the start of a race so that I would be coming up fast on the bridge when it was open, but the penalties for being over the line would be more severe in this instance. I came up with as much way on as possible, but as we passed under the bridge we lost the sidewind entirely and had only just enough way to take us through over the tide.

From the Medway we decided to take the first favourable wind over to the Essex shore, and despite a misty start we were soon out past the wreck of the *Montgomery,* and following the track of the Olau line ferry. We reached across to the Barrow, and then turned close-hauled down the Maplin channel. Now the wind let us down and headed us. Try as we would we could not get her round the Whitaker before the young flood made it impossible. There was nothing for it but to anchor close in to the sand and wait for the tide to ease or the wind to improve. We ghosted up the Crouch on the last of the flood and anchored by the mouth of the Roach.

Here was another river that was strange to us, although only a few miles away from the Blackwater. Burnham had a bad reputation, there were stories of being charged for anchoring, and the Crouch is a tricky river to sail into if you don't know it too well. But we found Paglesham a fine secluded anchorage, with some interesting walks ashore. We also overcame our fears of Burnham and sailed past and up to Fambridge where we visited a lobster farm and admired the old coaching inns on either side of the river. Here as elsewhere, we anchored clear of everyone else.

Although it looks as if the anchorage at Burnham left

no room to slide through at all, in fact it was wide enough for us to beat through and we found two sheltered anchorages one below and one above the town.

The time for the end of our holiday was nearly on us, and so was the time for decision making.

CHAPTER XX

Golden Anniversary

Privateer was fifty years old. That was something that had to be celebrated, and we had discussed her golden anniversary present for some time. One of my occasional crew who is a historian by trade tells the story of the famous 19th century journalist Mayhew. Someone was making him a cup of tea and counted the company present out loud before adding 'and one for the pot'. 'Ah I see' said Mayhew, 'It's the old story over again; doing something for ourselves, and making it out as if for another'. The presents we had in mind, it is true, were for our benefit.

For years we had maintained *Privateer* on a very small budget. Compared to the money spent on even quite a small racing yacht it was nothing of course; but it also compared favourably with similar boats of an older vintage. Boats built around the turn of the century are now beginning to show signs of old age, and we notice them regularly on the slip for replacement of planking, or worse. Our main problem remained the constant leaking through the stanchions and small spreads of rot in the covering board and top strake. This had become more serious, as the covering board on the port side had opened up a crack so that you could see daylight over the top of the top strake. This had given us a bad time crossing the channel in a blow when her deck was con-

167

On the left Pom, on the right Pete; two Dutchmen working in the mud at Maldon.

stantly under, and water was pouring in. The time had come to do something drastic about this and if possible stop the decks leaking once and for all.

I knew where to go for help; one of Will's fellow apprentices at Arthur Holt's had now set up on his own at Maldon, and we arranged to put *Privateer* in his care. Ralph came from a family of shipwrights, and in fact his grand-father had worked on the building of father's *Uldra* in Rowhedge. Ralph proposed a radical plan; to do away with the stanchions altogether and replace them with galvanised iron brackets. The stanchions were substantial pieces of oak that were fastened to all the grown frames and came up alongside them through the covering board, standing about six inches proud. These formed a firm support for the wash-strake and the capping above it. To take these out we had first to take out the covering board; Ralph recommended that we do this ashore, and it was arranged that we should go up to David Barke's yard, close to the Fulbridge at Maldon, where we could be lifted ashore by a crane. In the event, the crane never materialised, and the work was done down in the mud-berth. In the event also the work was masterminded by Ralph but actually done by two young Dutchmen, Pom and Pete.

Working on *Privateer* in the mud-berth was a mucky business for them, and though I supplied countless pallets and old water tanks for them to stand on, Pom and Pete were constantly being covered in mud and bringing it aboard with them. Despite this handicap they soon had the covering board off, and as is always the way with stories of repairs to old gaffers, it was immediately obvious that the top strake would have to come off as well. This, unlike the rest of the planking, was of oak, but there were many places where the rot spreading downwards had affected it, not to mention my crude patches over the years. We could now see *Privateer*'s timbers exposed for the first time. With the exceptions already mentioned and a couple of the half-beams which had gone, she looked very good, 'As good as when she was built' as Ralph put it. Taking out any plank is a lot of work, but the top strake is worse than any other as there are more fastenings to consider, and the chain plates have to come off as well. Pom and Pete struggled manfully with all this, meanwhile *Privateer* looked very sad and also rather small without any bulwark round her decks, and without her spars too. New Iroko planks went down for the covering board, and for the top strakes; we decided while we were at it to put in a mahogany rubbing strake which protects the outboard edge of the covering board. Ralph had worked out that it was impossible to re-use the old washboard and oak capping, so these were ditched. Then on went the galvanised brackets, each pair a slightly different shape so that they were square to the decking. The great advantage that these had over the old stanchions was that they lay on the deck and were bolted down through round drilled holes. There would be no movement and no opening up of a gap. Once the brackets were up the new larch washstrakes went up quickly and *Privateer* was beginning to look more of a boat and less of an old hulk. The last stage here was to bend the new mahogany capping round to bolt down to the tops of the brackets. This was a very tricky business and depended, amongst other things, on there being no faults in the grain of the long battens of mahogany. The starboard side went on the first time, but the port side split a couple of times before it was finally persuaded on. Pom and Pete worked like Dutchmen to complete the job, and I do not know who was most pleased when it was finished,

Galvanised iron brackets replaced the stanchions.

them or us. They had a boat shed on Osea Island and wanted to get on with building a Jol—a twenty five foot scaled-down version of a Baltic fishing boat.

In our haste, one job was left which should have been done then, but Pom settled that later in Heybridge Basin; it happened this way.

We had got to know Pom and Pete during this refit, and Pom had come sailing with us. He had come over to help me bring *Privateer* back from Ijmuiden where I had been compelled to leave her for a week or two. We had had a very calm and gentle passage all the way across to the Sunk off Harwich, when the sky started to blacken and a storm threatened. With the young flood tide sweeping us south we rounded the North East Gunfleet and turned up the Wallet. The black squall over Harwich came down over us and we were soon charging madly through the water with all the shore lights invisible, and with the driving rain making it impossible to see anything at all. With the tide under us we must have been making eight or nine knots over the ground. We had set a course down the middle of the Wallet, but if this visibility continued, and at this pace, we were going to run into something, whether it was the Gunfleet sand to port, the coast of Essex to starboard or the Eagle shoal ahead at the mouth of the Blackwater. Pom and I had a brief shout in which we decided that while it would be desirable to slow down a bit, it would not be easy to bring this about. We decided to press on and hope that the squall would clear. If we had shortened sail it would have made little difference to her speed and none to the problem. We were both highly relieved when the squall finally passed beyond us and we could see the lights of Clacton pier and later picked up the Knoll. We made a spectacular homecoming to the Blackwater, and as soon as we were safely inside we dropped the hook and hung out a light to get below; Pom refused my offer of a cooked meal, and we both lay on our bunks ready for sleep.

The rain was still pouring down, and a fair amount was dripping down on us as we lay in the bunks. I was used to this, and either arranged a towel over my head or lay askew to miss the drips, but Pom was outraged.

During the removal of the old top strakes, the tie beams had had to be cut, so these were now purely

ornamental and were not holding the shelf and the outside of the hull to the carline and cabin-top. We put
Privateer in Heybridge Basin, Pom put in some new tie-
bars and bolted them up tight. The decks were at last
held firm and it is now possible to lie in the bunk and
listen to the rain drumming noisily on the deck above
you without it weeping in your eye.

This completed the triumph of the refit, and the new
gleaming capping and rubbing strake gave *Privateer* a
very different appearance to the old, irregular and
patched-up bulwarks. She has made a definite move
away from being a smack and in the direction of being
more of a yacht, having always had some uncertainty
about her identity.

These major repairs and improvements were not the
only birthday present that we had in mind. During our
holiday in the Medway we had taken a long look at the
whole business of the engine. Considering the amount it
got used we spent a disproportionate amount of time
thinking about it, and putting in to Heybridge or Maldon
so that work could be done on it. Now was the time for
radical decisions if ever, and my first idea was to get hold
of an old Lister diesel and have it done up. I had worked
out that it would not need very great alterations to the
bearers to get this in the place of the Vedette, although
it would be a lot heavier and bulkier. Once again I started
reading Exchange and Mart, and it became clear that this
was going to cost quite a bit of money, allowing for the
reconditioning and for the changes that would be needed
for installation. About this time, our next door neighbour *Fearnought* had her fifty-year old Britt taken out
and a brand new Bukh put in its place. Mike Gibson
showed us his new engine and how easily it started.
Then we had met someone in the Swale who had installed

a new single-cylinder Yanmar the previous year. The discussion was moving on to new levels, and we were openly wondering if it was sensible to replace one second-hand engine with another. In other words, we had lost all grip on financial reality and were suffering an acute attack of dieselitis.

We went to talk the matter over with Mr French, whose marine engineering office overlooks the hard at Brightlingsea. I suspect he straight away diagnosed dieselitis, but treated us generously and helpfully. Then we went to see Mouse in Tollesbury, who had just completed installing the Bukh in *Fearnought*. The wheels were turning, soon *Privateer* was up the ditch and opposite Mouse's shed, we had collected the gleaming new engine from Brightlingsea, so small that it went in the boot of the car and so light that two of us could manhandle it.

Out swung the old Vedette, on its way to Maldon where I am sure its magneto, its brass carburettor, its reduction gear and other bits will be useful as spares. Mouse set to work on the Chinese puzzle of the bearers, which had to be moved sideways a few inches. All the cleverly concealed bolts were drawn and the bearers replaced without having to work through the hull; the old shaft and propellor could be used without any change (think what we are saving on that, we told ourselves) and so could the 3-gallon petrol tank under the deck. The new engine looked very tiny perched under the cockpit, and if we ever need to we can get at it from all sides quite easily. While Mouse was doing this skilled work and I was clearing up the shavings from the bilge, more skilled work was going on above us. A marine artist had set up his easel on the shore and had put *Privateer* in the middle of his canvas. When the tide came

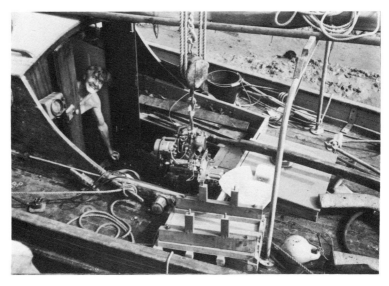

In swung the new engine.

in Mouse pressed the button and the engine started first time. It was the end of an era. For the first time in her fifty years of life *Privateer* had a brand new engine. We crept at slowest speed down the ditch and out into Woodrolfe Creek; when we got down to the Fleet we tried an experiment. It worked: we could now go astern.

So now at fifty *Privateer* has a brand new engine that works forward *and* astern, we have electrics like a mast-head light and navigational aids like a Patent Log; while the mahogany capping and rubbing strake gives her a new and unfamiliar look. Where will all this lead? We look back at years of ditch-crawling round to Pyefleet or Pin Mill, searching for clean shingly beaches on which to careen at the proper state of the ebb, all those days of ghosting in light airs in the Channel or in the North Sea, our antique jib goosewinging out on the tent-pole; or the times when we have been putting *Privateer* into a head sea in the Wallet or running down the rollers past a headland; the times we have tacked up the narrow channel to the mooring with tacks so short there is only just time to gather way before putting her round, the sunny days fitting out in Heybridge Basin or the wet nights when we huddle round the stove feeding it with driftwood. If we look ahead, will our life afloat be any different? Will all these improvements make our sailing less interesting and more predictable? Or will they open up new possibilities for us? Will we go on as before, but wondering however we used to manage without a Log, with decks that leaked, with nagivation lights that could not be seen and with an engine we could never depend on? We shall see.

APPENDIX

Privateer's first owner was H.A. Kemlo, an Ipswich solicitor. He has told the story of her building in the journal of the Little Ship Club.

In January, 1931, I conceived the idea of buying a smack yacht, and in the same month an advertisement, enquiring for a smack yacht and describing my requirements exactly, appeared in the *Yachting Monthly*. I wrote to the advertiser to know if he would pass on to me any replies that he had to spare, for I feared that, if I inserted another advertisement, owners of smack yachts would lose their enthusiasm for sending replies. The advertiser (although not a member of the Little Ship Club) turned out to be a keen yachtsman and a very decent fellow, and he not only acceded to my request but also told me that he knew of a good boat builder who would build a 10-ton yacht at the price of £100 for the hull and spars.

The idea that a yacht could be built at such a price surprised me, but the builder was spoken of so favourably that I thought it worthwhile to make investigations. I went up to Boston to have a look at the work he had in hand, and I got Mr Halliday to go up also, and he reported to me that the work he had seen—a 50-ft. smack nearing completion—was exceptionally sound both in materials and workmanship.

This report proved fatal, and I gave an order for the

building of a smack type yacht, 32 ft. L.O.A., at the price of £100 for the hull and spars—teak work extra.

The builder is Alexander Gostelow of Boston, Lincs. Gostelow is a thoroughly conscientious and able man, and has a high reputation in Lincolnshire and Norfolk. He has been building fishing smacks for many years, but of late conditions in the fishing trade have been so bad that he has turned to yacht building. Although Gostelow's own design is a smack type vessel, he is quite prepared, if he can be convinced that it is desirable, to vary his design within limits.

The low price at which Gostelow is able to build is chiefly due to the fact that he does the greater part of the work himself, with the assistance of his brother Herbert and nephew Tom. As a matter of fact, Gostelow tells me that the price of £100 which he charged me did not pay him, and in future he will have to charge £110 to £115.

The following is the specification of *Privateer:*

L.O.A.	32 ft.
L.W.L.	29 ft.
Beam	9 ft. 5 ins.
Draft	4 ft. 8 ins.

1. *Keel* of English oak, 4½ ins. by 8 ins. sided, 27 ft. long.

    Stem and sternpost, English oak, 4½ ins. thick.

    Deadwood, 5-in. elm.

    Heel knee and stomach knee grown oak crooks, 4½ ins. thick, through-fastened to keel, stem and sternpost with ¾-in. and ⅝-in. galvanised bolts.

    Keel plate, ½-in. by 4-in. wrought iron.

2. *Timbers.* Grown English oak, 2½ ins. by 2½ ins., spaced 17½ ins., centres with grown oak floors, 5 ins. to 9 ins., sided 2¾ ins. thick.

Steamed timbers, ⅞ in. by 1½ ins., one between each grown frame.

3. *Planking.* 1¼-in. best quality redwood up to bilge; above bilge 1-in. best redwood. English oak top strake.

4. Covering boards of 1¼-in. English oak.

Deck beams, 3 ins. by 3 ins., English oak.

Deck frames and carlines, English oak.

Grown oak knees on *all* beams, all galvanized bolted and clenched.

5. Decks of 1¼-in. by 3-in. best redwood.

Stanchions, rails, bittheads and kevels of English oak.

Cabin sides of teak, 16 ins. deep, on 1¾-in. frames and 1-in. top sides.

The whole throughout bolted to sawn oak carlines, 2 ins. by 3 ins.

Forecastle hatch and skylights of teak.

Galvanized nails used throughout.

All ironwork galvanized.

Mast, boom, gaff and bowsprit, Swedish poles.

Internal fittings of teak.

She has a straight stem and a counter of only 3 ft. in length. Her bows are comparatively lean and she has a clean and easy run aft; this, combined with a long straight keel, should make her a good boat before a wind and in heaving to. She has the bold sheer of a smack, but her freeboard aft is rather more than that of a smack of her dimensions. She is cutter-rigged and the distance of the mast abaft the stem is 11 ft.

Individual tastes in the matter of accommodation and fitting out vary so much that I will not give a description here. The cost of fitting out can, it seems, be almost anything, but I should say that, without an engine, the cost of building and fitting out, including sails, could, with care, be kept down to £200.

W.H. Johnston, of the Little Ship Club, has ordered a similar yacht, which is now nearing completion.

If any member would like to know more, or would like to see *Privateer,* I shall be only too pleased to hear from him (or her).

This account was first published in Coast & Country *and was based on the log of the voyage kept by Rex Pasley.*

DELIVERY VOYAGE
by Rex Pasley

Here's the logbook, one of many, its entries made in the usual bald fashion, leaving so much unsaid. A smudge here and there where a drip of water found its way on to the page; the ring showing where a mug of tea once stood. Re-reading the entries, it all comes back to me. . .

I had been asked to bring a yacht down from Boston, Lincs, where she had been built, to Fambridge in the River Crouch. The yacht, a cutter of nine tons T.M., had just been completed by a firm of smack builders and she was built on smack lines but with a well and rather more freeboard aft. Her name was *Privateer* and the year was 1932.

To catch the tide we had to get away promptly and had arranged for a tow down to the entrance and we parted company near the Roaring Middle Buoy at 2345 hrs. on 24 March. With the wind at SW. Force 3-4, we made good progress and by 0024 hrs. on the 25th we had the Lynn Light Vessel close abeam on the port hand.

The owner had arranged to come with a friend as crew, but by 0500 hrs. they had both retired below, overcome by seasickness. By 0625 hrs. we had the South Buoy abeam and shortly afterwards I set course SE. by S. with the wind heading us at SW. by S.

I had had no opportunity of checking the compass, but as there was no engine or other ironwork I expected little, if any, deviation and this was subsequently confirmed by a sun azimuth.

Conditions had so far been good, but the barometer had shown a tendency to fall during the night and, with some cirrus in the sky, it was possible the wind would back to the SE. and freshen.

The night had been cold. After about seven hours at the helm I would have welcomed a brief spell below, but the crew showed no inclination to move from their bunks.

As the coast was not visible, I decided to close the land in order to check my position, and at 1025 hrs. I came over to the port tack. The wind by now had backed to SE. though it was still little more than Force 4, but as it was nearing High Water we should have a foul wind and tide for the next six hours and should make little headway.

At 1210 hrs. we closed the land three-and-a-half miles South of Cromer and I stood out to sea again until 1345 hrs. With the wind at SE. Force 5 and with a head sea and the ebb running strongly, we closed the land off Mundesley, but we were now making virtually no headway.

It was about now that the owner appeared. Asking where we were he said that he had not only been very ill, but also had been unable to pass water and must see a doctor. This raised a serious problem. The barometer had dropped 0.19in. in the last four-and-a-half hours and, with the wind freshening this would become a dangerous lee shore. The nearest port was Great Yarmouth and to reach it would involve a long beat to windward against a rising sea and the possibility that conditions might be too bad to attempt the entrance. The alternative was to sail back to Cromer and anchor in the lee of the pier.

I explained the position, but the owner said that he could go on no longer and must go ashore, even if it meant endangering the ship. I therefore, under protest, closed the land and let go the anchor in two fathoms. Unfortunately, the anchor dragged and we had drifted into one fathom before we fetched up. I tried to get under way again, but the yacht paid off on the wrong tack and I had to let the anchor go again in a hurry. Fortunately, it held. I let go all the cable, 30 fathoms and stowed sail but still had some difficulty in getting the invalids on board the dinghy alongside owing to the sea.

When about to shove off, I noticed someone on shore signalling in semaphore I couldn't follow. As the seas were beginning to break near the shore, I signalled in Morse for a heavier boat to come out, but none was available.

So I started pulling ashore and turned the dinghy head to sea as I approached broken water. I then saw that there were a number of people ashore shouting encouragement and saying it was dangerous to land there! However, a coastguard waded out and hauled us in. We shipped a good deal of water, but landed in a comparatively dry condition.

While the crew went to see a doctor, I went with the coast-guard to give details which they then reported to Cromer.

We spent the night at the appropriately named Lifeboat Inn and at about 8 a.m. the coast-guard called and said that it was blowing strongly on shore and that he was afraid that the yacht would drive ashore and break up. He recommended that we should phone the coxswain of the lifeboat at Cromer to see if he could arrange for the yacht to be sailed back to Cromer as there was no hope of getting out in the dinghy.

Coxswain Blogg agreed to come away at once with a crew for an agreed sum of £10, which I thought very fair in the circumstances. Getting the anchor was a heavy job as the yacht was lying astern to wind and driving over it.

It was now nearly High Water and, with the anchor aboard and plenty of room to leeward, they were soon under way with the wind on the starboard quarter.

We then hired a car and drove into Cromer, where the owner went to the bank, to arrange for money and I telegraphed my wife in case an alarming account appeared in the Press.

It then had to be decided what to do next. It was obviously not desirable to leave the yacht at Cromer and I was asked if I was prepared to carry on.

As I had just spent about 16 hours at the helm without relief of any kind, and in view of the weather conditions, I said that I was prepared to do this only if a reliable hand could be found as crew. We put the proposition to Coxswain Blogg, who said he would see what he could arrange.

In the meantime he took us out to the yacht with a spare anchor to lay out in view of the weather. We found a lot of water on board as a result of seas breaking into the well when lying off Mundesley and it took some time to pump and bail out. Although the yacht must have bumped heavily on the bottom at low water, she was stoutly built and she did not suffer any serious damage. We also found that the bobstay had carried away because the eye plate on the stem, to which it was secured, had fractured. The starboard bowsprit shroud had also gone and this we renewed, but we could do nothing about the bobstay at the moment.

Later that day, Coxswain Blogg introduced us to one of his lifeboat crew, Jimmy Davies, who agreed to come with us. After arranging to meet at six the next morning, we spent the night at the Bath Hotel. As it was impossible to recover the dinghy we had arranged for this to be forwarded by rail.

After meeting us as arranged, Coxswain Blogg again took us out. Recovering the two anchors, we got under way under mainsail, foresail and No. 2 jib with the wind S SW. Force 5, gusting to 6 at times, and poor visibility.

By noon we had the Cockle lightship abeam. As the owner and friend were still suffering from seasickness it was decided to put into Great Yarmouth for the night. We moored to the quay below the bridge. When we left in the morning it was blowing quite hard from the SW. with a gale in prospect. Beating to windward in these conditions, we soon found that without the bobstay the bowsprit would not stand the No. 2 jib, which was the smallest we had. We hove-to inshore and took it in. Then we found that without a jib there was not power enough to drive through the head seas, which were now fairly steep, and at 1030 hrs. we put into Lowestoft to have the stem eye renewed and the bobstay replaced. We secured to the dolphins in the yacht basin and, with the help of Mr. Stigles, whom I had met before, the work was promptly carried out.

We cleared Lowestoft at 0815 hrs. the next morning and made good progress. By 1450 hrs. we had Orfordness Lighthouse abeam but by now time was running out as we all had to get back to our respective jobs and any hope of making Fambridge had to be abandoned. Conditions were not favourable for sailing to Harwich as the ebb would soon be setting in, and the only alternative was to leave the yacht at Orford.

Orford Haven, or Shingle Street, to give it its local name, is not easily identified from seaward and as the channel runs through shingle banks which are liable to change position a cautious approach is necessary until the leading marks on shore can be picked up. In poor visibility or, as I once discovered, when the sun is setting behind these marks, they too can be difficult to locate. The tide runs strongly through the channel and the best time to enter is on the early flood when the banks can also be seen. We on the other hand were coming in at about high water, not the ideal time to effect an entrance. At that time a pilot was available and, had I been alone, I should have taken advantage of this, but Jimmy Davies knew this coast intimately, and, as was to be expected was a fine seaman, and I was very happy for him to take us in. Seeing broken water where the seas were breaking over the banks he headed for these and, having found the channel and lined up the marks we were soon inside.

The last time I went in here there was no pilot but the Aldeburgh Yacht Club had provided a buoy to mark the entrance which greatly simplified matters.

It was a short sail up to Orford where we moored the yacht to two anchors and arranged for someone to keep an eye on her.

The time had now come to go our separate ways and to say good-bye to Jimmy Davies who appeared to have thoroughly enjoyed the experience and had proved a pleasant and cheerful companion. I was sad indeed to learn some years later that he had been drowned when coming ashore in bad conditions.

For me it was a great privilege to have the opportunity

of meeting Coxswain Blogg, a fine man with an outstanding lifeboat record.

As things turned out, it was not to be my last passage in the yacht for as the owner said that he would be happy for me to borrow the yacht at any time—in appreciation of my assistance—a very generous gesture that I was glad to take advantage of some time later.

I then sailed her to Holland and, after cruising in the Channel, I crossed the Thames Estuary to the River Crouch and so to Fambridge. The little ship had found her home at last.

She had proved a fine little vessel and, provided she was handled like a smack and not like a yacht, she would do anything you asked of her.

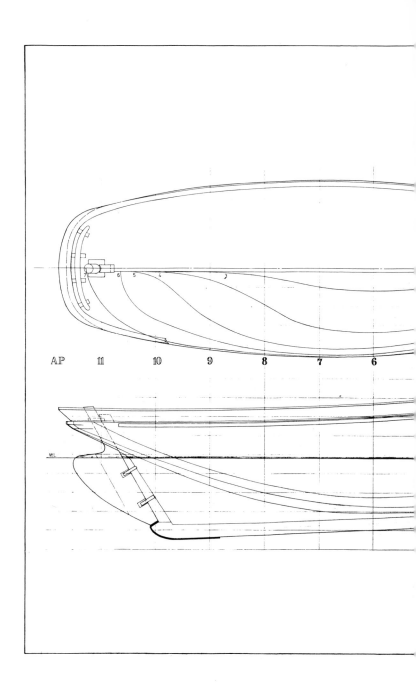

AP   11   10   9   8   7   6

WL

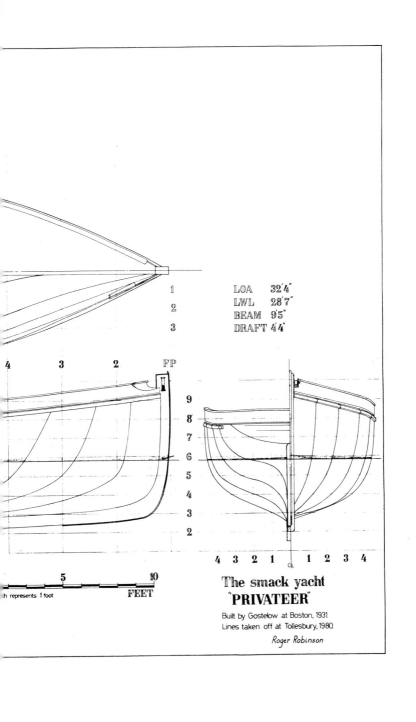

LOA   32'4"
LWL   28'7"
BEAM 9'5"
DRAFT 4'4"

The smack yacht
"PRIVATEER"

Built by Gostelow at Boston, 1931.
Lines taken off at Tollesbury, 1980.

Roger Robinson

Eastern Daily Press. 28~3~34

YACHT WITHOUT A CREW

MUNDESLEY MYSTERY SOLVED

A dandy rigged yacht, abandoned by her crew, anchored within 100 or so yards of the beach, aroused considerable speculation at Mundesley on Saturday morning.

The sea was very choppy with a strong S.E. wind, and there seemed every probability that unless her anchor held the yacht might be driven ashore. The mystery was solved later in the morning, when it was learned that the yacht was the Privateer and that the crew of three had come ashore the previous evening owing to medical assistance being required. Coastguards Shanahan and Breeds had the craft under observation throughout the night, and as there seemed little prospect, owing to weather conditions, of the crew returning, summoned for assistance from Cromer.

Soon after 10 a.m. a motor fishing boat, manned by Coxswain Blogg and three members of the Cromer lifeboat crew, appeared on the scene. After manoeuvring it in the rough weather the yacht was taken in tow.

The Privateer, which is of nine tons, is owned by Mr. H. Kembo, and the other members of the crew were Messrs. Cipasley and L. A. Crook. She left Boston, Lincs, on Thursday for Sandridge, Essex.

Shortly after 12 o'clock Coxswain Blogg and three members of the Cromer lifeboat crew, in the small fishing boat Britannia, towed the yacht to Cromer.

List of Owners

1931	H.A. Kemlo, Ipswich solicitor
1934/5	Nicholas Herbert
26th September 1935	William Whitworth, headmaster
28th April 1942	Charles Thomas) joint owners Alfred Spear)
3rd February 1950	Dr Dixon
16th February 1956	Leslie Potter
26th October 1959	Bridget Kinlen
8th December 1960	Henry Braine, Gravesend pilot
12th February 1962	Brian Jarman) joint owners Michael Pike)
2nd February 1966	Martin Eve

I REMEMBER THE TALL SHIPS

Frank Brookesmith

'Frank Brookesmith sailed on two of the last of the square-rigged ships to fly the Red Ensign. They were built to carry the maximum cargo with the minimum of crew. The work was hard, the food atrocious, the water in short supply and sometimes foul. The cargoes they carried were those that no other shipowners wanted to handle – rusty scrap-iron for Melbourne, evil-smelling bug ridden guano for the coast of Peru.' *Coast and Country*

'Frank Brookesmith has a flair for impressive, almost poetic description.' *The Nautical Magazine*

LAST OF THE SAILORMEN

Bob Roberts

Their tanned sails filling out in the breeze, their tall spars towering above other craft, the Thames barges were a familiar sight plying between London docks and the creeks and rivers of the East Coat and the Medway. These were the last sailing vessels to carry a commercial cargo, and the last of them all was the Cambria – skippered by Bob Roberts. Well known up and down the coast for his stories and songs, Bob recaptures here the life of a bygone era. He writes in the preface:

Much of this book has been written in a barge's cabin, rolling at anchor in Yarmouth Roads, storm-bound under the lee of the Yantlet Flats, waiting to load at Keadby or while lying idle in London River. I have not attempted to glorify or exaggerate this account of life in a type of sailing craft which is one of the most unique and efficient in the world. It is a life in which, to my mind, the pleasantness of a man's more sterling qualities, far outweigh the times of hardship and frustration.

First published in 1960, this is the first paperback edition, complete with the original photos and drawings.

CRUISE OF THE SNARK

Jack London

Jack London here writes of a true adventure – his own voyage across the Pacific in the 'Snark'. Knowing little of navigation, he set out from San Francisco to Polynesia and Melanesia with his wife and two crew, in a schooner whose defects included a tendency to leak and a refusal to face up to the wind when hove to.

'Written in the robust, racy style which made his other books world best-sellers.' *Yachting World*